HOW TO SURVIVE *and Thrive* AS A CHURCH LEADER

HOW TO
SURVIVE *and Thrive* AS
A CHURCH
LEADER

NICK CUTHBERT

MONARCH
BOOKS

Oxford, UK & Grand Rapids, Michigan

First published in the UK in 2006 by Monarch Books
(a publishing imprint of Lion Hudson plc),
Mayfield House, 256 Banbury Road, Oxford OX2 7DH
Tel: +44 (0) 1865 302750 Fax: +44 (0) 1865 302757
Email: monarch@lionhudson.com
www.lionhudson.com

Distributed by:
UK: Marston Book Services Ltd, PO Box 269,
Abingdon, Oxon OX14 4YN
USA: Kregel Publications, PO Box 2607,
Grand Rapids, Michigan 49501

ISBN-13: 978-1-85424-761-2 (UK)
ISBN-10: 1-85424-761-1 (UK)
ISBN-13: 978-0-8254-6125-5 USA)
ISBN-10: 0-8254-6125-1 (USA)

The text paper used in this book has been made from wood
independently certified as having come from sustainable forests.

British Library Cataloguing Data
A catalogue record for this book is available
from the British Library.

Printed and bound in Great Britain by Cox & Wyman Ltd, Reading

Contents

Dedication

To my fantastic family, Lois, Andrew and Mark who have shared this adventure with me. Thank you for all your love, support and friendship.

To the people at Riverside, who for 22 years have been our other 'family'.

Foreword

There's a lot to be said for simply "lasting" – for staying the course, continuing faithful, remaining on board when the rats are leaping off the ship.

Living in a day in which the only publicity the church gets is either reports of phenomenal achievements or dismal failures – of fast-growth churches or leaders falling prey to sins of the flesh – we could all use a dose of honouring just plain steadfastness.

Nick Cuthbert and his wife Lois have lived that word in a way that helps define it, and here he is sharing a few life-lessons he's learned on how to keep your head above water when the floodtide hits. I encourage your taking time with what he has to say – encourage you to do so for three reasons.

First: Because the Bible calls for the kind of leader who stands firm. "Be steadfast, unmovable, always abounding in the work of the Lord, knowing that your labour is not in vain in the Lord!" (I Cor. 15:58, NKJV). It's the character trait that demonstrates the shepherd's heart and the servant's dependability. Like a shepherd's constancy when wild creatures attack, or like a servant's fidelity even when he is unnoticed, you and I as believers in Jesus are called to live that way: steadfastly!

Second: Because we live in an hour that cries out for Christians who will stand their ground, notwithstanding the withering assaults of hell, the passive indifference of the world, the critical spirit sometimes shown by fellow workers or the wearing, self-demeaning assessments of our own mind when discouraged. Voices from every direction including within are too often responded to as the decision-maker on our worth. But steadfast resistance will be found where we tune into the affirming voice of the Holy Spirit, whispering hope, deepening confidence and settling anxiety or self-doubt.

Third: Because you are herewith being introduced to a seasoned and proven leader who is providing you with immensely practical, purpose-driven wisdom. I've known Nick Cuthbert for over twenty-five years. To my mind, he characterizes the rich combination of the leader who blends the timeless and the contemporary in a way that produces fruit – the fruit of spiritual substance and the fruit of spiritual results... that last!

So welcome to a handbook that will serve you well; one that will contribute to the kind of life Jesus described as "putting your hand to the plough" and keeping the blade pressing through the turf, even when the dust is blowing in your face and the weather reports tell you it's useless to labour that hard just now. Kingdom people stay on track, blade to the ground, and the results will always be the same: they reap a harvest.

Sounds like a fourth reason for reading this book, now that I think of it.

God bless you as you do!

Jack W. Hayford
President, International Foursquare Church
Chancellor, The King's College and Seminary

Introduction

Even though I don't sit easy with the title of this book, I believe it is the right one! Leadership, or any other calling in life, shouldn't be a matter of survival. It should be enjoyable and fulfilling and, like everything else, when it comes to an end, celebrated and rejoiced over.

But that is not the way it is for many people. The church is full of men and women, in 'full-time' ministry who would love to change their job for another. There are many who have left, disillusioned and worn out. Some have left because of foolish behaviour and some through sheer tiredness. The question is, "Did this need to be so?" Maybe a new generation of men and women are coming along who will heed the warnings, learn to pace their lives and fulfil their calling with joy and satisfaction. If this book is any help at all in this, it will have done its job.

After all, the calling to be a leader in the church is one of the greatest privileges in the world and is, in the main, a wonderful way to spend your working life. But it is hard. I am very glad that that is what I have spent most of my life doing, but I know it is not easy.

It is all too easy to tell yourself, "I shouldn't feel like this," when you are tired and worn out. Many people in secular employment may look at those in full-time ministry and wonder what they do all day. If you sense that people are thinking that way, you may find yourself working all hours to somehow prove to them that you really do work hard.

There are reasons why "the ministry" as we know it today is hard. Let me mention a few things that make it difficult to survive.

A lack of boundaries

Many people, even if they work long hours, know when their working day starts and when it finishes. In ministry, that is rarely the case. You may have a rough pattern of life but the "people game" is not neat and tidy. People don't have problems to order. Many times people need to be seen at their convenience, not yours. Very often it is unpredictable as to when your day starts and when it finishes.

Having no weekends off for year after year seems normal but is a huge loss. A day off in the week is good, in fact, essential, but it isn't the same as a weekend. Try a weekend away some time and you will wonder why you never experienced one before!

A lack of clear boundaries is tiring and the more we can do to put them in place the better, for us and our family's sake.

Poor pay

I have not yet met a pastor who felt he or she was overpaid. In fact, some situations in the UK have been downright unkind and wrong, but ministers feel they are unable to complain as this would be deemed unspiritual. I know some are well looked after, but for the many that aren't, when the going gets tough, you may wonder why you do it. It certainly isn't for the money! Money is more than the stuff itself as it represents something greater. Generosity expresses value, whereas meanness expresses a lack of being valued. It isn't just the amount of pay that matters. What is meaningful is that people want to bless you.

Discouragement

Discouragement is a killer! Jonathan Edwards (the 18th century preacher, not the athlete!) used to say that the greatest attack on leaders came through discouragement. Accomplishing a task is very encouraging for most people and finishing a task is fulfilling. The "people" business, however, means that the task is never complete. The job is never fully done. Of course there are great encouragements when people make strides forward, but there is plenty to knock you back.

If something goes wrong, the leader takes the flak, and there is always someone around to criticize. However much we might deny it, negative comments do hurt. People can be critical even when everything goes well, when you would expect the opposite to be true, that the leader would receive some praise! I am afraid that for many, that is not always the case. Criticism without praise is very discouraging.

Loneliness

Leadership can be a lonely place. Most senior church leaders have found it difficult to have friends in the church. Indeed, many have been taught not to develop friendships with people they are leading and discipling. Things are better now in many situations and some great teams are made up of people who are real friends. But chat to most leaders and they will talk to you about the sense of isolation they feel. The church family can, for the leader, be a strange place where he/she feels cut off from everyone. How much more do leaders need friends outside the church who understand what they are going through? Few men in particular have close buddies, which is a serious problem.

The pressure to be perfect

It may well be very difficult for the person who is leading, preaching, and encouraging others, to see himself (or herself) as a fellow traveller with them because he/she perceives a pressure to be a perfect example of the Christian life. Everybody else is allowed to fail, but not the leader.

Working with volunteers

When almost everyone a church leader works with is a volunteer, it brings with it a whole set of joys and difficulties. The negative side is that nobody has to do what they are asked to do. They are not paid to do it, they are not in danger of losing their job, and they often feel they are doing the leader and the church a favour.

And with all of this we so easily become serious! I have been much helped by Jerry Cook, an American pastor and friend, who is perhaps best known for a book that has revolutionized many churches through its simplicity and honesty: *Love, Acceptance and Forgiveness*[1]. Out of his own experience of breakdown and ill health, he wrote another book with the great title of *A Few Things I've Learned Since I Knew it All*[2]. In it he describes the dangerous trio of Busy/Important/Serious whom he sees as three invaders who hang out together and so easily take over our lives. We will look at the first two later in this book but at this point let him describe his fall into "seriousness", which he does in the form of a poem (or parts of it) that he wrote to his wife.

He introduces his poem by saying, "Like a virus, seriousness affected my entire being. Fun, spontaneity and life and laughter, feeling unwanted and unwelcome, slipped quietly away. The precious things tiptoed out of my life lest they distract this busy and important man from doing God's serious business. I began to realize how long they had been gone and how much I had missed them. I tried to write about it."

Laughter,
Not strained or shallow.
Fun laughter, it sort of bubbles out, easy, smooth.
The kind that people have when they are enjoying
Not anything in particular, everything in general.
A being-together kind of laughter.
Somewhere... sometime... somehow,
I traded "being" laughter for "doing" laughter.

Then...
I got serious.
Life got serious.
Demands, supposed omnipotence.
The universe surely required my involvement to survive!
And "being" laughter slipped away, like a shadow.
It slipped past me
And walked on with my baby girl
(Fathering a perfect child can be a serious business).
It walked on with my Love
(Being head of the house and priest in the home and spiritual
leader and final authority and...
It's serious business you know!)

And my children laughed,
But not with me.
"He's tired"... "He's sick"... "He's angry",
He's gone away into his own lonely, serious world.
A world of "doing" laughter,
A world of objects and duties
And calendars (God curse them!)

And things, problems, expectations.
Airports, motels, conferences, jet lag,
Endless introductions.
And the children laughed as they grew
But I was doing important things, and missed them.

My Love laughed,
But not with me.
"We must be serious in the presence of this great man
about such magnificent things."

At the end of the poem, which continues with a hope of change, Jerry Cook shares how God freed him to discover "being" laughter again. It is this ability to know "being" laughter that all of us need to discover if we are not only to survive but also to thrive in church leadership.

A personal story

"What do you do for a living?" enquired the Italian doctor, as he looked down at me lying on the trolley in the outpatients department of the hospital on the Venetian Lido. I felt awkward telling him that I was a pastor but when I did, he looked a little surprised. His assumption had been that I must be involved in what he would have considered a stressful occupation. I don't think that "pastor" quite fitted the bill! After all, weren't we meant to be some of the few people in society living free of stress, especially as we only work one day a week?!

I had been suffering from a vastly increased heart rate for a few days and it had come to a head here in Venice on our 25th wedding anniversary. Lois was so worried about me that she had ordered a taxi and taken me to the nearest hospital.

Nobody seemed to speak any English so we managed to communicate using a rather comical sign language, until an English-speaking nurse appeared. As well as speaking good English, she happened to be extremely pretty, both of which facts I was grateful for, but the latter may not have helped my heart rate!

"Well," said a cardiologist who just happened to be passing through and who had a smattering of English, "there is nothing wrong with your heart as such; what we have seen on your ECG is caused by stress. You had better go home and sort things out." He injected me with a beta-blocker drug which had the immediate effect of bringing my heart rate down to normal.

A few months previously, I had become aware that something was wrong when I was away on a retreat with a group of guys. This event has been a regular part of my life for over 20 years. My friends and I go away for two days, three times a year, to share where we are at in life, and pray for each other. It is a great mixture of quite deep sharing and much laughter and fun.

On this occasion, when it came to my turn to share, I tried to recount how I was, but without any warning, I broke down in tears and found myself saying repeatedly, "I can't go on any more." I wasn't sure what I meant by that but something deep was going on inside me. I hadn't planned to say anything but in this place of trust and safety, what was really going on came flowing out. I realized that although I could try and pretend, in reality I was at the end of the line and had run out of emotional reserves. If somebody had suggested two weeks' holiday as a remedy, it wouldn't have done the trick. I needed something much more profound than that.

I made a commitment to my friends to see a counsellor and a medical doctor. In fact, I'd already talked to a doctor friend of mine some weeks before and had told him that I felt tired the whole time and had lost enthusiasm for much of what I was doing. He told me that he thought I was depressed and that I needed to look for the cause and do something about it.

In the following weeks I did both the things I had committed myself to do. I began a very helpful series of counselling sessions with a couple that helped me unpack some of my emotional issues. I knew that I still had unresolved issues from the past relating to my mother, who was ill for most of my childhood, and also from the fact that I had gone away to school from the age of eight. Lois, who is also a counsellor, had already helped me greatly with a number of these issues, but I realized there was still much to do. It was in those sessions that I began to understand that much of my sense of significance and self-worth was tied up not in God but in Christian ministry. I had been working not only to serve God but to feed many inner needs and now I could no longer go on.

My visit to the doctor proved reassuring but he underlined what my friend had felt. Before he even examined me he said, " I am sure I will find nothing physically wrong. My guess is you are doing too much of the wrong things and it has reached a crisis point." He was right!

At this point, as I began to think about making changes in my life and wondering what the way ahead was, we were preparing for two major events in our lives: our 25th wedding anniversary and the celebration of 25 years of ministry in the city of Birmingham.

On a Thursday night in late April, we had a marvellous dinner party in a local restaurant, a place that had become a favourite of ours over a number of years. It was so good to be with family and our closest friends. Many heart-warming things were said and we felt very blessed by all those nearest to us. On the Sunday of the same week, I preached at our two morning services (why, I do not know), and in the afternoon we had a large tea party with many more friends and some folk from the church. Lois and I renewed our vows to one another, which was a very meaningful time. We went straight from there to a fantastic celebration of 25 years in ministry, which I led. Many people who had worked with us over the years came back for the occasion and wonderful stories were told of God's goodness to us all.

After all the activity of the day, I was on adrenaline overload.

We were to fly out to Venice the next day (the reason for going right away was that we had got a cheap deal, which was an understandable but foolish way to make the decision). Our friends, Graham and Jill, drove us the two-hour journey that night to a hotel near the airport. All night I felt a little odd and was unable to sleep properly. The next day we took the train to Gatwick and on arrival at the airport, I felt unwell. We called for the airport nurse who examined me and said my blood pressure was high and my pulse rate far too fast and that I should consider not going on this trip. After some consideration, however, we all agreed that the holiday might be good for me and once there I would be able to relax.

It was an awful journey. We collapsed into the hotel room and all that evening and throughout the night, my heart rate would not slow down. Lois tried to stay calm but the next morning, when I was still feeling ghastly, she said, "That's enough. We're going to the hospital!" Fortunately, it was only a short taxi ride away. Trying to explain the problem to people who did not speak English, along with the concern about feeling very ill in a foreign country, made the experience all the more traumatic. Wonderfully, as I have mentioned, it turned out that a visiting cardiologist was in the hospital that day and, much to my relief, he spoke English. Meanwhile, Lois was enduring her own trauma not knowing what was going on, as they hadn't allowed her in with me. What a way to celebrate our 25th!

We had a funny few days in Venice. I went around very slowly as if we were on our 50th anniversary, feeling very odd, but at least knowing all was reasonably OK and trying to make it a good celebration for Lois. At least it was memorable! Two days later, we touched back down at Gatwick and both burst into tears! It was so good to be home.

That was not the end, as months of tests ensued to check there was nothing else going on. I have a family history of heart disease and that added to the concerns. After a very frustrating time with local doctors, a friend who is a consultant in another area of medicine telephoned and said, "I hear you haven't been well. Ring Pat; she's a consultant cardiologist and a Christian, and ask if she will see you." I rang her expecting to be put on a waiting list for months, but when I told her what was going on she said she would see me three days later and cleared some space to do so. I owe Pat an enormous debt of gratitude. She knew right away that this was not a problem with my heart, but nevertheless did the tests to reassure herself and me. Most of all, she helped me see that I had to straighten my life out and that I had been fortunate to have a warning.

What was interesting was that when I told people, "I must make changes because of stress and burnout," it received a great deal less sympathy than, "My consultant says I have to do this!" Stress has almost become something to be proud of in our society, and overwork a sign of how great you are.

What was happening to me was the early stages of burnout. The incident in Venice had been part of that and had been brought about by a season of stress. Stress and burnout are two separate things but I had been experiencing the effects of both. Stress was affecting me because I had not learned to control and monitor my adrenaline levels; the burnout symptoms were the result of years of build-up.

I am so grateful that I have come through that experience without a complete loss of health and ministry, at least thus far. For many, the realization that something is wrong comes too late and the long-term repercussions are severe.

Although this book is not intended to be a biographical account of our life and ministry, a brief outline might help to put what I am writing here into perspective. Lois and I moved to Birmingham in the early part of 1972. As you will see, much of what we have been involved in over the years would be deemed by others to be "successful" and so they might easily wonder why I should have ended up needing help. The truth is that a breakdown has little to do with the work you are involved in, but is primarily to do with what is going on inside you. It is related to your particular drivers. I am a child of my generation and of my particular background and parenting. In order to keep healthy you need to understand yourself and the things that cause you to do what you do. No two people are the same. Often it isn't until you get into midlife that the cracks begin to appear and by then much of the damage may have been done. It is never too late to be healed, though, or at least for the healing process to begin.

I came to Christ in my last year of school through the witness of a friend and the ministry of an Anglican minister called David MacInnes. After three years at university and then at Bible college, I was invited to Birmingham to be involved in a city-centre youth work that didn't at that point exist except in the mind of David and the purposes of God. Lois and I married and moved to a city that neither of us knew. We had no income, so trusted that God would provide.

There was no job but we believed the work would open up. It began with following up a few young people who had been converted through a recent evangelistic event. As we did so, by arranging teaching meetings in the Cathedral with David, the work exploded, so much so that hundreds of young people were coming week by week. Over the course of five or six years, hundreds, possibly thousands, of them found Christ or were encouraged in the faith. For me this experience opened up the world of university missions and other youth events. We, and the great team we worked with, were permanently out of our depth but, in spite of ourselves, the Lord seemed to go on blessing. It wasn't all easy. There were many struggles over finance, relationships, and the sheer frustration of working with volunteers, but somehow the sense of things happening made up for many of the difficulties.

That period of our lives came to a close. As it did so, the church began. We had no intention of starting a church, but there was a lack of spiritual life in our locality and we needed to have some fellowship. We found it with a small group of friends. As we met each week, the small group got bigger until the house could not contain us all and we moved to a school. We realized, rather reluctantly, that we were becoming a church. And so the Riverside (as the church became known) adventure began. It doesn't sound a very dramatic start, does it? Sorry, but that is the way it was. In fact, as I grow older, I am aware that so much of God's leading is like that. You get on with life, keeping your relationship with him as good as it can be, and somehow you find yourself in the will of God, a fact that is confirmed often only by the twist of circumstances.

Over the last 20 years or so, we have met in every shape and size of building, experimented in style and emphasis, been in and out of being the flavour of the month, had a huge turnover of people due to the transience of city life, and experimented with leadership patterns. It has all been a great adventure and the source of great joy as God has brought some wonderful people into our lives to work with us, on staff or as members of the church. We have known pain too, through people behaving badly, people we love moving away, and our own foolishness. The church has grown to become one of the larger places of worship in the city and in many people's eyes this would be deemed a success, but when you are close to something, you rarely see it as that. We have learned a huge amount along the way and consistently been aware of the grace of God. We wouldn't have missed it for the world.

For the last year, we have been in the process of handing over to younger leaders, which is proving very challenging and very rewarding. But that is another story.

Each of the chapters in this short book represents an area of leadership that I wish I had taken more seriously many years before. It is only now that many of these lessons are being applied in my life. Although this book is about my own personal experience, my hope is that there will be principles that apply to you as well. I trust that is so.

All the chapters are short and each ends with some questions to think about. You might find it helpful to take a chapter a day rather than read the book in one sitting.

Notes

1. Jerry Cook and Stanley C. Baldwin, *Love, Acceptance and Forgiveness,* Ventura, Regal, 1979.
2. Jerry Cook and Stanley C. Baldwin, *A Few Things I've Learned Since I Knew it All,* Nashville, W Publishing Group, 1989.

Chapter 1

Receive significance from God

"There is no limit to what you can achieve if you don't mind who gets the credit." So said Mark Twain. But like so many truisms, it sounds fine until you have to put it into practice. Unless we go for the underlying issue, there is no point in even trying to put it into practice. I want to start here on the vital issue of "significance" because it is the area that stood out so starkly for me when I had to face key issues in my life.

This is a major issue of our time. It affects everyone to one degree or another because, in a world that has rejected God, the need for significance is not being met and therefore people today are trying to find it wherever they can. The pressure to look the right shape, wear the right clothes and own the right things (fed in all of us by the hugely powerful advertising industry) is at the heart of Western society.

The question, "How do you do?", is quickly followed nowadays by the question, "What do you do?" The present world system values people by what they do, what they own and, to some measure, particularly amongst the younger generation, by what they wear. We find ourselves describing people to others: "He's a brain surgeon, you know," and then we wait for the sharp intake of breath indicating how impressed our listeners are. "He's a bus driver" never seems to have the same sort of effect! We peer into the passing Rolls Royce to see who is driving it, but the Nissan Micra goes by unnoticed.

Even though we have put our lives in God's hands, it is all too easy to keep on looking for significance in what Jeremiah called "broken cisterns that cannot hold water" (Jeremiah 2:13). Christian leaders slip into this tendency unless they take steps to deal with it. Leaders are unlikely to get much recognition for their money or clothing if they are clergy, and they are often no longer held in high regard in society. But we long to have recognition and so the success of our church work becomes incredibly important. You may be slow to own this, so just for the moment assume that it is my problem only!

The most obvious sign of my need for significance was in the area of numbers of people who attended my church. Credibility can be counted in numbers! Consider this typical exchange:

"And how many are in your church?"

"Well, if everyone turned up with their families, about 17."

"Oh!"

"And how many are there in *your* church?"

"Well, somewhere around 5,000 but it's difficult to count exactly because it's growing so fast."

"Wow!"

We may not consider the fact that the first person questioned here is working in a very tough inner-city area, while the second person has gathered people from many other churches because they have a great building and many middle-class young people. Who is successful? The second, of course. We talk of such a leader as a "significant pastor" and feel he should be treated with respect and a sense of awe. A great man is in our midst! And how I wanted to be a great man!

So what were some of the things that I began to observe about myself that I would have to do something about?

- At lunch on Sunday, I would complain about the people who were not at the morning service. I rarely seemed to notice who *was* there, but became annoyed by absence.
- If anyone left the church, I felt depressed and even angry (as if it was a personal attack on me).
- If we had friends visiting, I found myself saying, "Of course we normally have more people than this but some are away on..."
- I became very sensitive to lots of small things that I felt were not done right.
- I reacted to criticism in a way that was out of proportion to what was said.

My reaction to situations tended to demonstrate the attitude: "I need this thing to work! It may not be important to you but it is to me."

On my travels, people often asked which church I belonged to. When I said, "Riverside", I realized that most people had never heard of it! How was it possible that something so important to me and so successful was not the talk of the entire nation? Why was I not known as the pastor of this incredibly vital and strategic work? What seemed so important to me was so seemingly unimportant to everyone else! I find this true everywhere. I talk with men and women who work all hours of the day and night, neglecting their families and their health for the incredibly "important" work they think they are doing when, in fact, from an outsider's point of view, their behaviour is extraordinary because it all seems so unbelievably unimportant.

The issue is that the importance of your work has to do with the level of personal significance it gives you. If your significance is tied up with your work (whatever it may be), then you will find yourself driven to "succeed" to make you feel good about yourself. It is a sad fact that most pastors, when looking at models to learn from, choose those that are beyond their attainability. So what happens? A pastor of a small rural church sees a church of 15,000 members and tries to learn from it. But, in fact, everything shouts at him that he is a failure, and so he sets himself up for discouragement. Of course, we all need things to aim for or we will never grow and develop, but so often we set ourselves up to fail because the targets are wrong.

It is worth noticing that in the natural world, some flowers are large and some are small. Who wants a garden full of primroses that are three feet tall? Who expects a rose to be two inches above the ground? It is the variety of size and colour that makes a garden so beautiful. So why have we bought into the "big is beautiful" philosophy of the Western world?

I am part of the generation that came out of the revolution of the 1960s. This era produced a generation of entrepreneurial leadership. However, one of its weaknesses was an obsession with success. Many of those leaders, and I would include myself, came from a background of unaffirmed fathering, which produces a strong need to find significance in what a person achieves. I would like to hope that the next generation of leaders will find a greater sense of peace in "being" and not just "doing".

I had to come to terms with my own misplaced sense of significance in achievement, and the truth that it was other people who were able to control whether I felt significant or not. I had put great power into other people's hands.

A management training consultant writes,

Let me quote from Christopher Banks, hero of Kazuo Ishiguro's *When We Were Orphans*, "But for those like us, our fate is to face the world as orphans, chasing through long years the shadows of vanished parents. There is nothing for it but to try and see through our missions to the end, as best we can, for until we do so, we will be permitted no calm."

This "orphan spirit" is a spirit of drivenness – the attempt to justify our existence and prove our acceptability through achievement and activity. It leads to an unending cycle of grief – unending because no achievement or amount of activity can fully justify our need for acceptance.

In our society, increasingly "you are what you do (and get paid for)". We all too easily draw our identity from our work, and our need to succeed in this context (particularly as many jobs are currently under threat) creates a drive to be accepted. We may talk about wanting to get off the express train of Western society, but the reality is that we are afraid – afraid of being a nobody. Who are you, who am I, when we stop? Until we find a satisfying answer to this question our hurry sickness will persist.[1]

Of course she is right. The tragedy is that such an attitude affects Christian leaders as much as everyone else.

The solution for me was to re-engage with the love of God. I needed the Holy Spirit to begin a fresh work in me to reveal that my significance came from being a child of God. He loves me, accepts me and is totally committed to me whatever I do or do not do. My significance in his eyes is far more important than anything I receive from another person. I began to see again, for myself, truths that I had taught others but was failing to grasp fully for myself, and it was incredibly liberating.

This new insight did not take away my passion for church growth and effective ministry but I began to rejoice in a new way in everyone God brought to us. It was still sad when some people left the church but the old pain was gone. I made a point not to talk about sizes of congregations with other leaders unless it was relevant. Instead I began to rejoice in the variety.

If church and its ups and downs means too much to you, it may mean you have misplaced your significance and security. Repentance (a change in thinking) and renewal of your acceptance of the unconditional love of God are the ways forward. Insecurity is primarily the fruit of not knowing the unconditional love of God. It is easy to preach about the love of God but until it has broken through in glorious revelation in your own heart, you will always flail around, unsure of where to find your significance.

We are made for relationships and we have a God-given desire to achieve and do something worthwhile in our lives. Both these things rightly make us feel significant, i.e. that we have a valid place on the earth. But we cannot afford for either relationships or achievement to be the primary source of our sense of significance, value and security. You cannot hope to survive Christian leadership if you do not know deep in your innermost being that your security and significance lie in the personal love of God, the heavenly Father.

When it doesn't matter who gets the credit, you know your sense of worth is derived from the right source.

Stop for a moment and consider:

1. From what source do I get my sense of significance?
2. Do I know deep within that God loves me unconditionally?
3. Do I need to seek counselling to work something through?
4. What steps will I take to move from the idolatry of ministry to putting God at the centre?

Notes

1. Beverley Shepherd, *Women in Work*, LICC Seminar, 2003.

Chapter 2

Reject busyness and "hurry sickness"

A s I sit down to write this, I have an email that I need to reply to that says, "Thank you for agreeing to come to our event, especially as I know how busy you must be." It could also have read, "Thank you for agreeing to come to our event, because we know how important you are!"

Much of my life in church ministry has been characterized by being busy. I assumed that that was a mark of doing a good job. The funny thing is that I can remember in the early days in Birmingham when we were involved in a thriving youth work, we were often surprisingly "unbusy" and yet very fruitful. I realize now how unnecessary "busyness" can be. In fact, life can be full without being busy. Busyness is not just a statement about your diary but also about your mind.

Jerry Cook, quoted in the introduction, says in the same book, "Important people are always busy. They rush from somewhere to somewhere else. Wherever they are, is typically on the way to where they are going, to some destination that is never quite clear but always more important than here. I am also deliciously aware that others are saying with admiration, 'He works so hard. How can he possibly accomplish so much? He is certainly a great man of God.'"

This problem among leaders is often demonstrated for me at conferences. Some speakers will come and go, only staying as long as they need to deliver their talk. They are too important to stay and listen to the context of what they are

29

contributing to. And it is rare to be at a leaders' conference and not have a whole crowd leave early because they have "more important things to do".

Eugene Peterson in his excellent book, *The Gift*, says that the word "busy" linked to the word "pastor" is a betrayal and should cause us to react as we would to the word "adulterous" attached to "wife", or "embezzling" to describe a "banker". He is in fact talking specifically about the role of pastor but it could well be applied to all forms of Christian leadership.

He gives two reasons for busyness. (Be warned, as it is a bit of a shock when you first see the truth of this). The first reason is vanity. The long hours, the crowded schedule, the full diary all speak of importance. If I want to be seen as important, I don't want to appear inactive or not in demand. You see, busy people are important people, and so to feel important we must be sure to be seen to be busy. It is a pattern that many of us fall into because we have accepted the relationship between "busy" and "important". We assume that others might interpret our unbusyness to mean that people don't want us or that we are lazy.

The second reason that Peterson cites for our busyness is actually laziness. His reasoning, by means of uncomfortable logic, is that if we allow others to dictate our diary, we are in fact lazy. Instead, we are to take control of our lives and decide for ourselves what we will do and what we will not do. We do not have to give in to every demand and approach on our time. The busy person may well have allowed other people's priorities for his or her life to win the day. Even in the business world, there is serious doubt as to whether long hours and overcrowded schedules actually achieve more, but the Western world has bought so firmly into this notion that most are trapped by living on an ever-faster spinning wheel, as it were. It takes a great deal of courage to be the one to call a halt to it.

The sad fact is that in a world where most people are stressed and worn out by the pace of everything, many pastors and Christian leaders, rather than being a haven of calm for other people, are themselves caught up in the same whirl of busyness. They may be that way because being the opposite fills them with guilt and challenges their self-worth. I know because I struggle with this dilemma.

You may have had the experience of travelling on the motorway, then stopping for a coffee and looking out of the restaurant window in amazement at the speed that everyone is going. Then you finish your drink and slot right back in. That is exactly what many of us do in life! Is it time to take the lead and get off the fast track?

In the same book, Eugene Peterson gives a most helpful picture. He writes,

> In Herman Melville's *Moby Dick*, there is a turbulent scene in which a whaleboat scuds across a frothing ocean in pursuit of the great, white whale, Moby Dick. The sailors are labouring fiercely, every muscle taut, all attention and energy concentrating on the task. The cosmic conflict between good and evil is joined; chaotic sea and demonic sea monster versus the morally outraged man, Captain Ahab. In the boat, however, there is one man who does nothing. He doesn't hold an oar; he doesn't perspire; he doesn't shout. He is the harpooner, quiet and poised, waiting. And then this sentence: "To ensure the greatest efficiency in the dart, the harpooners of this world must start to their feet out of idleness, and not out of toil."

Stop reading for a moment and think about that. Remember the words in Isaiah 30:15, "...in quietness and trust is your strength, but you would have none of it." The natural tendency for all of us is to assume the role of the oarsman as well as the harpooner. We want to be where the action is and to be seen to be doing something. But someone must throw the harpoon and he or she must do it out of a place of rest.

So often, the illustrations Jesus used of ministry had to do with the quiet and the small. They were farming illustrations such as sowing seed or pictures of home life. Often the small, insignificant thing done in secret and calm produces the significant and remarkably fruitful result.

It has often struck me as interesting that a church will go through a period known as an "interregnum" (the term in itself says much about how we view leadership!) when one leader goes and another has not yet arrived. In some situations this can last as long as a year. The remarkable thing is that during those times so many churches seem to do extraordinarily well. Then the new person comes and before long is working like crazy, having been handed all responsibility. How come everyone managed when he/she wasn't there, and why could the leader not slide in almost unnoticed, let the people continue in their roles, and just be there to "throw the harpoons" (not a metaphor for attacking people but for strategic work!)?

The work of prayer and preaching is much more effective when we come from a place of quiet. A good and effective sermon is not usually produced out of mere study and by collecting good illustrations, but out of a settled and prayerful heart that is able to reflect the place of peace from which it comes. As mentioned later, we are at our most creative when least stressed.

I once heard a friend describe the difference between the African view of time and the European view. I don't know if he was right but he suggested that African people see life as a series of events. When these are done or attended to, the rest of the time is for "being". But in the West, time is there to be filled. Hence the vast array of material on "time management", a concept which somehow suggests that we are accountable for every second and that every moment should contain something worthwhile. None of it must be "wasted". Is that really what life is about? I suspect not.

"Hurry sickness" is a common bedfellow to the "busy" syndrome. That is my experience, anyway, and may be for you too, especially if you are an A-type personality. I once heard a guy say, "I realized how caught up I am with hurry when I continually flush the toilet before I've finished!" I immediately knew that was also me, and so I tried to stop it! It was amazingly difficult. You feel the need to do something while you are standing there! (The women reading this will not be able to identify with that. If they can, they are in serious trouble!)

Very often when my wife, Lois, and I are out shopping with the purpose of spending some time together, I will say to her, "Look, I've a good idea. While you go to this shop, I'll go and get this and that, and we'll meet up later. It will really save time." Thankfully she rarely agrees with these "time-saving" antics. Saving time is not the issue on a day off. It has something to do with enjoying being together! I eat too fast, talk too fast, walk too fast and live too fast. I have spent much of my life living a step ahead of myself and not enjoying the moment. It is a recipe for burnout and I do not want to go there again.

The Red Queen in *Alice in Wonderland* said, "Now here, you see, it takes all the running you can do, to keep in the same place. If you want to get somewhere else, you must run twice as fast as that."

"Hurry sickness" could be defined as the struggle to achieve an ever-increasing amount, in an ever-decreasing time frame. If we live like that, we'll end up "skimming" at most things and, most importantly of all, our relationships will suffer.

The belief system that causes this problem is, "We don't have enough time." We live under the illusion that time is a scarce commodity. I've already mentioned that we have even created an environment where if someone has "time on their hands" they are deemed less important. Someone has rightly observed that this belief system "boosts the credibility of things that happen quickly. It infuses with wonderful new prestige any new time-saving device. After all, who needs such a device? People who have no time! And who has least time? The best people!"[1]

We serve a very generous God and he doesn't short-change us on time. Jesus always had time. He was never in a hurry. He walked nearly everywhere. Can you imagine how much more he could have achieved if he had driven a four-wheel-drive, or used email, a mobile phone and a personal digital assistant? What a shame he had none of those things! He could have squeezed the equivalent of five years' ministry into three! And what on earth was Paul doing "wintering in Crete"? What a waste of an entire winter! Did he not know there was a world to win? They seemed to be sauntering around with none of today's sense of shortage of time. Did they achieve much less?

Do you think God gives us twice as much to do today because we have all the technology? Do African Christians in their slower way of life receive half the directions for their ministry than those in the West? It certainly makes me think we may have got it wrong somewhere, but who will dare slow down?

God is not in a hurry. Hurrying is a human characteristic. You may remember the line of the popular song by Simon and Garfunkel that says, "Slow down, you move too fast. You've got to make the morning last." Bear in mind that you can't go faster than someone you are following. We are hopefully trying to follow Jesus and he isn't running anywhere!

To get free from hurry sickness takes serious training. It was suggested to me that I should pick the slowest queue in the supermarket, the slowest lane on the motorway, and so on for a period of time, in order to adjust my whole system to a new way of living. I am learning this new approach and I certainly feel better for it and, do you know, I think I get at least as much achieved.

If you want to survive leadership and be in it for the long haul, I suggest you find a way to slow down and, in your heart, deal with the need to be busy.

Stop for a moment and consider:

1. **How do I feel when others consider me to be busy?**
2. **How will I become "unbusy"?**
3. **What practical and achievable steps can I take to deal with "hurry sickness"?**
4. **If I only did one thing today and did it well, what would it be?**

Notes

1. Michael Lewis, *Forbes ASAP*, Nov. 1995.

Chapter 3
Look for obedience before success

In my desire to find out more about leadership, I was interested to read the biography of a man who had taken over an already high-achieving company and turned it into one of the biggest and most profitable corporations worldwide. It was apparently a story of success but it left me feeling a bit cold and asking the question, "So what?" This man's broken marriage was passed over in one page as if it was incidental to the real stuff of making money. When he left, the company struggled to maintain what he had achieved. There seemed to be poor succession planning. Was this success at all?

We live in a world in which "success" is highly prized. And this is subtly a part of the Christian world as well. It is very easy to find yourself looking for "it", but the very illusory nature of what success really is, means your pursuit of it will continually make you feel you are a failure.

So many people have spent their lives climbing the ladder and at the end of the day they find it was up against the wrong wall! The wall is labelled "success" and the view from the top can be very disappointing in the light of the effort to get there. In modern terms, Jesus would not be termed a success in his lifetime. He never travelled far enough to make a global impact. He never wrote a book. He ended up with eleven committed people (or possibly 120 if you count those at Pentecost). He built no building, created no organization and made no money.

But he did what he came to do. And that is the key. He faced all the pressures to be a success, but chose another way.

The problem lies not in the concept of success but in how it is evaluated. If success means achieving what you set out to achieve, all well and good. The opposite of success is failure and nobody wants to fail in what they set out to do. But if success means reaching a certain level of size, wealth and celebrity (the benchmark of which is set by society – or worse, by the church) as the point to reach, then we have embraced the worst form of idolatry. Most books on leadership are about how to be a success. Money, size, influence and prestige are seen as the important values of the Western world.

But is Christian leadership about success and failure? I suspect not. Certainly not on these terms, yet so much of present Christian culture has bought into this understanding that it is almost taken as normal. (Please do not infer from this any criticism of large churches. I am thrilled that as part of the body of Christ large congregations are being raised up. I believe that the church should be growing, which for some will mean getting larger, and for some, planting new works.)

Paul describes himself as a servant before calling himself an apostle. Now, the role of a servant is very straightforward and it is possible to assess whether you have been a good or a bad servant. In Paul's day a good servant did what he or she was asked to do and a bad servant didn't. It really was as simple as that. Servants were not primarily entrepreneurs but carried out the orders of others. Now, you could argue that the parable of the talents suggests personal initiative, but actually it is about obedience. The master was saying, "I have given you various gifts, now use them fully." Obedience here means doing something with what you have got. The man who was reprimanded was the one who was disobedient.

At the end of our lives we all hope to hear the words, "Well done, good and faithful servant." In other words, the issue as far as God is concerned is not what you have achieved in terms of results but whether you did what you were equipped and asked to do.

When I was at school, I played the second horn in the second orchestra. There was no third horn and no third orchestra, which meant that as far as horn players were concerned, you didn't get any lower. The only way for me to go was up! I have to admit, for most of the time, I felt a total failure as a musician. At the beginning of a concert, everybody applauded the conductor and then the leader of the orchestra and finally any soloists. I never received individual recognition. It was never expected that any special adulation would be given to the second horn (especially in the second orchestra!).

The parts I had to play were pretty dull and much of the time was spent counting. At one rehearsal, I felt so surplus to requirements, I pretended to play but didn't! Immediately, the conductor stopped the playing and said in a loud voice, "And where is the second horn? Don't you understand that the composer needed the second horn to play its part? It won't sound as he intended without it. For your benefit we will begin again!" Actually, I think if the composer had heard me play the second horn part, he might well have felt it was better without it!

The point is that the orchestra was "successful" because I was obedient to my part. History is silent over a vast array of "unsuccessful" people without whose lives much of what we do would not be possible. The world is full of "successful" people without whose success we might all do just as well.

Was David Livingstone a success or a failure? If you read the story of his life in Africa, it is obvious that if he lived today we would not rate him highly as a missionary in terms of evangelistic results. As an explorer, we might give him some acceptance. Yet is it possible that his obedience to a call from

God laid the groundwork for much of what is happening in the African continent today?

If you read too many books, and look at too many videos and Christian magazines, you can quickly feel as if you are achieving very little. Many books read by Christian leaders are accounts of apparently successful churches where the definition of success nearly always has to do with size and influence. However, there is a new generation of younger leaders who are not impressed by all of this, and that is good for the future.

At a recent conference I attended, the speakers were all given glowing introductions to prepare us for the obvious privilege of listening to them. The main things said about them were either a list of qualifications attained or colleges attended, or the size of the church or organization that they were now running. The implication was that these were highly successful people, so by listening to them maybe the rest of us could be successful too.

A leading agent for celebrities in Britain was quoted in the press as saying, "I have worked with a large number of extremely successful people but I would have to say that very, very few were happy." Maybe their ladders were up against the wrong wall after all. I think I would rather be obedient to Christ and hear his words, "Well done!"

In his poem "*If*", Rudyard Kipling sums much of this up:

If you can keep your head when all about you
Are losing theirs and blaming it on you,
If you can trust yourself when all men doubt you
But make allowance for their doubting too;
If you can wait and not be tired by waiting,
Or being lied about, don't deal in lies,
Or being hated, don't give way to hating,
And yet don't look too good, nor talk too wise:

If you can dream – and not make dreams your master,
If you can think – and not make thoughts your aim;
If you can meet with Triumph and Disaster
And treat those two impostors just the same;
If you can bear to hear the truth you've spoken
Twisted by knaves to make a trap for fools,
Or watch the things you gave your life to, broken,
And stoop and build 'em up with worn-out tools:

If you can make one heap of all your winnings
And risk it all on one turn of pitch-and-toss,
And lose, and start again at your beginnings
And never breathe a word about your loss;
If you can force your heart and nerve and sinew
To serve your turn long after they are gone,
And so hold on when there is nothing in you
Except the Will which says to them: "Hold on!"

If you can talk with crowds and keep your virtue,
Or walk with kings – nor lose the common touch,
If neither foes nor loving friends can hurt you;
If all men count with you, but none too much;
If you can fill the unforgiving minute
With sixty seconds' worth of distance run,
Yours is the Earth and everything that's in it,
And – which is more – you'll be a Man, my son!

(**my emphasis**)

Whether you are a man or a woman, if you follow this advice you will find peace and freedom and something of what God has for you. Who knows, you might be deemed a success by all around you, but you will handle it lightly, recognizing that it was a gift from God. You will never survive leadership if your life is driven by the desire to succeed in this world's terms, but if you seek to be obedient as best you can, you may be surprised at what you can do.

Stop for a moment and consider:

1. What am I chasing after and why?
2. What has God called me to be and do, and I am being obedient to this?
3. Where have I felt the pressure to be a success and how will I let it go?
4. What are the simple marks of obedience in my life that bring peace?

Chapter 4

Don't sweat the small stuff

When I was going through my "difficult time", an evangelist friend sent me a very helpful book on life change. Inside the front cover he had written, "Don't sweat the small stuff. It's all small stuff!"

At the time, I did not realize that this was the title of a very popular book by Richard Carlson, which consists of 100 short chapters, each one underlining an area of "small stuff" that we take too seriously. In the introduction to the book Carlson points out that this problem is primarily an issue of attitude. He writes,

> When we are immobilized by little things – when we are irritated, annoyed, and easily bothered, our (over)reactions not only make us frustrated but actually get in the way of getting what we want. We lose sight of the bigger picture, focus on the negative, and annoy other people who might otherwise help us. In other words, we live our lives as if they were one big emergency! We often rush around looking busy, trying to solve problems, but in reality, we are often compounding them. Because everything seems like such a big deal, we end up spending our lives dealing with one drama after another.[1]

Stephen Covey has a lovely expression: "being deep in the thick of thin things". Life is full of "thin things", all of which can consume you and fill your days.

The Duke of Wellington was no stranger to small stuff. He wrote a classic letter to the War Office:

> Gentlemen: Whilst marching to Portugal to a position which commands the approach to Madrid and the French forces, my officers have been diligently complying with your request which has been sent by H.M. ship from London to Lisbon and then by dispatch rider to our headquarters. We have enumerated our saddles, bridles, tents and tent poles and all manner of sundry items for which His Majesty's Government holds me accountable. I have despatched reports on the character, wit, and spleen of every officer. Each item and every farthing has been accounted for, with two regrettable exceptions for which I beg you your indulgence. Unfortunately, the sum of one shilling and nine pence remains unaccounted for in one infantry battalion's petty cash and there has been a hideous confusion as to the number of jars of raspberry jam issued to one cavalry regiment during a sandstorm in western Spain. This reprehensible carelessness may be related to the pressure of circumstances since we are at war with France, a fact which may come as a bit of a surprise to you gentlemen in Whitehall. This brings me to my present purpose, which is to request elucidation of my instructions from His Majesty's Government, so that I may better understand why I am dragging an army over these barren plains. I construe that perforce it must be one of the alternative duties, as given below. I shall pursue one with the best of my ability but I cannot do both. 1. To train an army of uniformed British clerks in Spain for the benefit of the accountants and copy boys in London, or perchance, 2. To see to it that the forces of Napoleon are driven out of Spain.

When you and I read of the great exploits of Wellington and his victories over Napoleon, I doubt we are aware of the terrible blunder over the raspberry jam and I imagine we are rather glad that he got his priorities right. What is the "raspberry jam" in your life? What are the things that cause you irritation, annoyance and sleepless nights? Do they really matter in the context of what you are meant to be doing?

Most of the stress points in my life in the church have been over what was actually "small stuff" but appeared at the time to be "huge stuff". I remember once hearing a story about a break-in at a large department store. When it was discovered the next day that there had been intruders in the night, it was both a surprise and a relief to find that nothing had been stolen. But as the day passed, chaos reigned in the store. Whoever had broken in had changed all the price tags on the items. The expensive items were now dirt-cheap and the cheap items expensive. You can imagine how much disorder was be created by such a simple act!

For many of us the price or value tags have actually been turned round in our lives. What is actually unimportant in the long term seems at the time to be of huge importance and the key issues go unnoticed. When I look at some of the things that week after week caused me to get "my knickers in a twist", I am learning to ask such questions as,

- "Does this really matter?"
- "In five years from now is this going to have made any significant difference?"
- "In the light of eternity and issues of life and death, where does this rate in importance?"
- "Is the damage to my well-being, my sense of peace and ultimately my health worth the internal hassle I am putting myself through?"

To most of those questions there is a resounding "NO". As the well-known prayer says, "Lord, help me to change the things that can be changed, accept the things that cannot be, and have the wisdom to know the difference."

It takes a fresh attitude and presence of mind to stand back, take a deep breath and say, "This is small stuff and I will not get into a sweat about it. Some things might not get done, but life, as we know it, will go on." You will be all the better for being at peace and letting it go, rather than running round like a scared rabbit with your internal state sinking into chaos. The truth is that most of our pressures are small stuff and we are called to get on with the important things. Often the mass of small stuff so fills our minds that we forget the thing we were actually called to do!

Some months ago, we visited a church where the minister was a young man who had been part of the church here in Birmingham. He looked a bit surprised when we walked in but it did not appear to put him off his stride. It was a great service and he preached excellently. Afterwards, as I went to tell him how much we had enjoyed being with them, he was quick to apologize for a whole lot of things that were not as he would have liked them. "This building isn't very good. The chairs were out of order. The children were noisy. The band was a bit out of tune, etc., etc." As he spoke, I heard myself! None of those things had bothered me in the slightest that day. In fact, the rather chaotic, laid-back feel of the service had been rather endearing. For him, though, the small stuff had seemed so important. And for years, I had felt the same way he had. Of course, it is important to do things well and make a place of worship as inviting as possible. It is not a question of whether these things should be done but whether you let them take up too much importance and so enhance their ulcer-inducing qualities.

"And it came to pass..." is a great biblical phrase. Most things come to pass or rather come *in order* to pass. They don't matter that much and should be treated lightly. There is a job to be done but, for so many in the ministry, life is filled with issues of "raspberry jam" and it is easy to lose sight of our original calling and the priorities that made that possible. We may look with envy at the apostles who decided to "give themselves to prayer and the ministry of the Word". But we need to follow their example and determination as they sought to get their priorities right. They found people to do the other important work who were more gifted at it than they were. This is not always easy to do, especially in a small church, but at least an attempt should be made.

Leadership survival is rarely dependent on how we deal with the big and important issues but how we deal with the mass of little things that are thrown at us each day. When we are tired, these things loom so large in our lives, and it is difficult to see them in perspective. It is the accumulation of the small stuff that will eventually bring us down, not because it is there but because it causes us to "sweat".

Stop for a moment and consider:

1. **When did I last get annoyed and irritated, and how important was it?**
2. **How am I going to spot the small stuff and how am I going to treat it?**
3. **What is it that I need to stop sweating about today and get into perspective?**

Notes

1. Richard Carlson, *Don't Sweat the Small Stuff,* New York, Hyperion, 1997.

Chapter 5

Never dwell on regret

I don't know if you have ever played golf. I do play, although not as much or as well as I'd like to. In my worst moments, I used to describe myself as a "hacker", which is a technical term for "someone who can get from the tee to the green without ever touching the fairway"! I've convinced myself that I would play well if I were to find the time to do it more often. One thing that I notice about golfing talk is that it nearly always starts with the words, "If only..." "If only I had taken a different club..." "If only I had not lifted my head..." "If only you had told me about the river in the gully..." "If only the ball had not hit that branch it would be on the green by now."

The strange assumption is that "if only" I had done something different, I'd have played a brilliant shot and everything would be fine now. I have to say that most of the golfers I know would still be in a mess but just a different one!

When the children were young and Lois could not travel with me, it meant that I would travel to speaking engagements on my own. On the way home a cloud of depression would sometimes settle on me as I began to find something to regret in what I had just done.

Even if I had decided what I thought was the right thing to speak on, I would often have a few alternative ideas in my mind. I would deliver my message, which was usually well received by the people. Then I would set off home and I would begin to think through what I had said and, more importantly, what I had failed to say. My mind would begin to go into a spin of regret and self-condemnation. After a time this was so consistent and happened so often, that I began to dread my return journeys. I soon developed a habit of putting the radio on loud and immersing myself in the music so as not to think about what I had been doing until I could be more rational about it. Subsequently, travelling with someone else I could laugh and talk with has proved a great help. But I had to undergo a very real inner change, which the Spirit helped me make.

What I am writing about here may be peculiar to me but I somehow doubt it. I have battled with regret for much of my life and it is only recently that I have really taken it in hand. I could regret anything from clothes I had bought, restaurants I chose, even meals I selected, to holidays I had booked. The alternative to what I chose to do often seemed far better than what I actually ended up doing. I hope you have never behaved in such an extreme fashion but most of us are to some degree held back from a hopeful future because of a wrong attitude to the past and often by the regret of decisions made.

This is a very serious disease because it forces you to live both in the past and in unreality. It fills you with a sense of guilt and failure that traps you into not moving forward in the present and enjoying the reality you are now in. This is a major handicap for a leader and needs radical surgery.

Such a mindset can lead to a form of depression. There is no positive value in it whatsoever, as the past is the past and can never be recalled. You cannot go back in time and change things. It is totally impossible, so why even contemplate it? It is a waste of time and energy. The problem with most regretting is that it happens in the privacy of our own thoughts and therefore becomes so utterly destructive.

Of course, we need to be secure enough to look at choices we have made and face up to the possibility that they were not the best, learn from it and move on. Where we have done or said things that we should not have, and these have hurt other people, there needs to be proper apology and restoration. Where we have wilfully disobeyed God, there must be repentance and the receiving of forgiveness. But that is quite another thing from the worrying, debilitating effects of continual regret.

At the heart of the issue is discovering the amazing grace of God in our lives. Let me illustrate it in the following way. It is becoming increasingly common to have a satellite navigation system in the car. This device is particularly useful if your job requires you to travel to many new places. It means you don't have to stop and look at a map all the time. If you don't have such a device and you are trying to follow a map, and you take a wrong turn, you have to turn around and go back to the point where you went wrong, particularly if you are following someone else's instructions. The great thing about "Sat Nav" is that when you fail to follow the instructions you've been given by this very calm female voice, you expect to be told off! You might be expecting the words, "You idiot! I told you to turn left and you went straight on! How do you ever expect to get to your destination if you cannot obey simple instructions?" But, no! What you get is a period of silence and then the calm voice again, completely unruffled, giving you further instructions as if nothing had happened at all. She quietly redirects you onto an alternative route.

In other words, she starts from where you are, and takes you from there to where you are meant to be. This is an incredible illustration of God's grace toward us. The truth is that we do get things wrong, we do make poor judgements, we do go off course, and we do act foolishly, but it is never final. God has a most extraordinary way of taking us from where we are, without flap or panic, and directing us back to where we should be. We get there in the end!

I now know I have a choice. I can choose to go with the decisions that I make and even if they are not perfect, enjoy the present circumstances I find myself in. After all, I only get to live today once, so I might as well enjoy it while it's there. I am challenged by Paul's statement, "forgetting what lies behind, to press on..." But it is a choice, and it has to made constantly, if we are not to be robbed of the sheer joy of living every day in a place of contentment, "in whatever circumstance I find myself". A good rule is to admit mistakes, apologize where necessary, learn what you need to, and move on. Do not live in the past.

We can spend our time and energy wishing we had done things differently, wishing we could have the last years over again, or we can find a place of peace where we are. In that place, we can look into the future, knowing there is Someone who has a far greater desire for our welfare than we do, who will get us there in spite of ourselves.

Some years ago, after we had gone through a painful time in ministry and I was wondering if the joy would ever return again, I felt a profound sense of helplessness and hopelessness. This was coupled with serious regret over some decisions that had been made and even doubt as to whether the years given to Christian ministry had been worth it. When you get into a negative cycle of thinking like that, it is difficult to get out of it and I was struggling.

Around this time, we attended a conference in the USA with some friends. In one service, we had a long time of worship (which I did not engage with very well), followed by a talk which I am sure was good but it went past me. At the end, Jack Hayford, who had been involved in the meeting, went to the piano and said he felt he should sing a song for some people in the meeting. As he began to play the plaintiff melody, the words touched us both at a deep and profound level, melting away a long period of discouragement:

> What was lost in battle,
> What was taken unfaithfully,
> Where Satan has planted his seed,
> Where your health is ailing,
> Or your strength is failing,
> I will restore to you all of this and more,
> I will restore to you all of this and more.

> > I will restore, I will restore.
> > I will restore to you all of this and more.
> > I will restore, I will restore,
> > I will restore to you all of this and more.

These words, which Lois scribbled down as Jack sang, have stayed in her handbag for years and we have often stopped to read them as a reminder of the Lord's touch on our lives. Thank goodness, he is a restoring God. It was not only an attitude of regret that had caused my pain; there were other issues, but regret was certainly part of the problem. There is no way we can survive leadership if we live in regret or even allow it a foothold in our minds.

Don't regret the past. It is of no value to do so and it will only make leadership survival more difficult. God is a restorer, so let him restore. Enjoy the day. Look to tomorrow with hope. If there have been mistakes, let him restore to you all of this and more!

Stop for a moment and consider:

1. What part of the past lives in me as a place of regret?
2. What have I learnt from it?
3. What active steps will I take today to move on from there?
4. How am I learning to discipline my thinking to prevent a slide into despair?
5. Can I see the hand of our loving God moving me on from where I am?

Chapter 6

Function in your strengths

Some time ago I received the following in the post:

The results of a computerized survey indicate that the perfect minister preaches for exactly 20 minutes. He (or she) condemns sin but never upsets anyone. He works from 6am until midnight in pastoral duties and also acts as church caretaker, administrator and music leader. He is happy with the £60 a week the church pays him, and he gives £50 to the poor. He is trendy but ordinary, extravert and introvert, jovial and serious.

He is 28 years old, speaks fluent English, Greek and Hebrew, and is an experienced and gifted speaker. He is excellent with the elderly, relates well to youth and has a deep understanding of family issues. He spends most of his time relating to those outside the church but is always available in his office when needed.

If your minister does not measure up to these standards, simply send this letter to six other churches who are ready to change theirs.

Then bundle up your minister and send him or her to the church at the top of the list. Within twelve months you will receive 1,643 ministers. One of them should be perfect.

WARNING: Don't break the chain. One church failed to pass the letter on correctly and got their old minister back in six weeks!

Unfortunately, this image of the all-singing, all-dancing leader is not a thing of the past but is still the expectation of many. It is the cause of a great deal of weariness. One of the most important things I have done in my life was to come to terms with what I was not good at and realize that that was OK. An unwritten law says that leaders are good at everything and therefore expected to be multi-talented. In this way, we are set up to fail.

We are all designed to be part of a community of people who need each other. This is the great richness of being part of the human race. In order for us to work in cooperation with others, we are all created differently and are designed with limitations. These limitations are not part of our fallenness. It was always meant that way so we would need each other. The lead violinist is not a failure because he cannot play the drums. A doctor is not a failure because he cannot build a house. A goalkeeper is not a failure because he cannot score goals. When everyone does what they do well, the orchestra sounds terrific, the sick get helped, the houses are built and the team wins the game.

Well, that is the theory, but something tells us we ought to be able to do everything. So what happens? The things we do well get scant attention and are squeezed into a small amount of time. Our limitations get most of the attention, because our inability to do these things well means they need more time and effort.

And what are we criticized for? Rarely for operating in our area of strength but usually for what we don't do well! Why should that be? We were simply not designed to do well in that area. None of us likes criticism, however, and so to avoid it we may well work hard to shore up the areas of our lives where we have limitations.

And what causes the majority of stress in our lives? Doing

the things we are not good at. If you give yourself to what you are gifted at, however hard and long you work, even if you are physically exhausted by it, it is very unlikely it will cause you stress. In fact, it will be life-giving and invigorating. But give even a short time to your area of limitation and you will be tired and stressed very quickly. As I shared earlier, much of my stress came from doing things that I was not gifted to do. It was alright for a time but needed to come to an end.

What happens in many professions is that people who are excellent and gifted in what they do are promoted. With promotion come extras to the job, often an added load of administration. Hands-on people usually struggle with administration and therefore give extra time to it, with the result that they neglect their area of strength. They then get criticized that their "admin" is poor while at the same time the area of their strength is suffering.

I heard recently of discussions going on in a leading bank in the UK that went something like this: "Why do we keep promoting people to their level of incompetence? The reason is because we value them and promotion means more money. Why don't we increase pay for people who do what they do well and let them stay at the level that best expresses their gifting?" A novel idea indeed! It would lead to both happy employees and a successful company, as everyone would be functioning in their strengths. I wonder if they will have the courage to see it through.

Now, it needs to be said that there are times for all of us to do what we do not want to do, and so we should be prepared to act at such times. There is also a time for learning new skills, as it may be that some areas of apparent weakness are only due to lack of training.

But what about you and I in our leadership roles? The first stage is to discover who we are and how we have been wired. There are plenty of good schemes around for doing that. One way is to sit down with the people who know us well and ask them what they see our strengths to be, what we could be better at with help and training, and what are our areas of non-giftedness. Then we need to be freed to pursue our strengths. If that means the people are not there to fill the gaps, it may well be that the world will still go on until the right person comes along.

Most church leaders I meet are seriously stressed and stretched and I suspect a great deal has to do with living under a false expectation, and the pressure of doing what they *can* do but *should not* be doing. You will never be happy or fulfilled until you let it go and if by some chance the world collapses, so be it, but I doubt it will! Very often, if you stand back and create a gap, someone with the gift may well come out of the woodwork.

I had a problem with believing that anyone could honestly enjoy things like administration, so I thought that I should grin and bear it. Then to find people who not only did it well but also thrived on it was beyond comprehension and a joy. If you are in the fortunate position to be able to add to your team, try to add people in your weaker areas and it will help free you. (Very often administration is the first point of need.) At the end of the day, what leaders have to offer is leadership and that should be their primary contribution – unless, of course, leadership is not actually your gift. In a recent survey in the USA, the majority of pastors interviewed did not believe they had leadership gifts. How stressful is that! This finding is underscored by the following.

In the USA publication, *Christianity Today*, in August 2002, an article was published entitled, "The third coming of George Barna". Barna is and has been one of the best-known statisticians in the field of church life. The article revealed that after ten years he had come to the conclusion that much of his work with leaders was flawed. He said this: "The strategy was flawed because it had an assumption. The assumption was that the people in leadership are actually leaders. I thought that all I had to do was give them the right information and they would draw the right conclusions. Most people in positions of eadership in local churches aren't leaders. They are great people, but they are not leaders." Barna recognized that these are admirable people whose gifts lie in Bible teaching and pastoral care. These are valuable gifts, but they are not leadership. Leadership means the ability to motivate and lead change.

Because the models set up in front of pastors and leaders today are predominantly entrepreneurial models, if you are not a leader in that mode, you will always feel under stress and have a sense of failure. The question seriously needs to be asked, "Is this model really valid or have we bought into it because we are a success-orientated generation?" Entrepreneurial leaders will produce mega-churches because that flows from their gifting, but we had better be careful before we promote that as the preferred or even the biblical model.

The key to all this is for us to come to terms personally with our own gifting and be comfortable in our own skin. If we have only limited leadership gifting, we must either be content with that and look after the people God has given us, or we should look for people with leadership gifts to work alongside us. This may well be why the early church had apostolic gifting overseeing the wider church, with pastors caring for the "church that meets in the house of..." We have become so nervous of the term "apostle" that we have avoided the issue that it raises: that of a leadership role apart from "pastor".

Barna concludes rightly, "What I am saying is that they

need to understand what God designed them to do in ministry, and not try to do something that God didn't call them to be." It may well take humility and wisdom to point out to a congregation that you are a pastor and that you need to find a person with leadership gifts. That person could well be a non-ordained staff member. They don't even have to be full-time or paid and could even offer their gift from their place of work.

Remember, at the end, you will not have to give account for what you were *not* given but for the gifts you *were* given. If you spend your life trying to be something you are not, you will never survive. Also if you fail to recognize those who have different gifts from yourself and let them function, you may never see fulfilled all that could be done.

It will be very difficult to survive leadership if you are trying to function outside your God-given gifting.

Stop for a moment and consider:

1. **Do I know what mix of gifts I have been given?**
2. **Am I using and developing those gifts as a number one priority?**
3. **What gifts do I need to look for in other people to complement me?**
4. **What today will I decide to stop doing?**

Chapter 7
Put family first

Here is one man's account of his downfall:

It all started so innocently. Here I was, doing God's work. I was happy. I wasn't looking for an affair. But it happens to pastors, and the results can be devastating. I saw a real need. My pastor's heart responded to her needs. My efforts on her behalf were met with warmth, understanding and acceptance. I felt needed. I saw in her eyes sparks of excitement for my godly attention, and it felt good. It was innocent and well-meaning, not intended to foster an affair.

It was good to be appreciated. The bottom line was that she made me feel important. No, I did not want to be unfaithful to my wife. True, our marriage wasn't as exciting as it had been earlier. My wife and I had got involved in different interests and activities. Our time schedules were so full that we hardly saw each other, and when we did we were both so tired that it was flat – no excitement.

But with her it was different – electric, powerful, energizing.

Then there were the kids. My own kids were doing well in school. Her kids? Little support, massive needs, lots of hurting. After all, my kids have a mother even if I am not there.

Slowly, the "friend" became a mistress. There were the extra hours of counselling that couldn't wait. There were more and more "evening opportunities" that took me away from home. I could sense my wife's anxiety and puzzlement, but I kept spending time with "her". My spouse kept quiet about what was going on, but I could detect a smouldering resentment that drove us even further apart, and made my contacts with "her" even more desirable to me. It was easy to rationalize that if my wife were more attuned to my needs, I might spend more time at home.

Soon I noticed a subtle shift in my own attitude. At home I was a husband and dad. That's fine, I guess. But with her I was a hero! She appreciated everything that I did, and looked at me with loving, longing, unquestioning eyes. I enjoyed spending time with her. She fed my ego and I craved her delicacies.

One day she called me and gave an open invitation: "I know this may be hard for you, but I want you for a whole weekend. It's a little place up in the mountains, and honestly I need you. No one else will do. Please say yes!" Her voice was plaintive and sincere. Heady stuff, this. When did my spouse last make such a clear invitation and show that same eagerness to have me with her?

I knew I should have said no, but there was a part of me that needed the recognition. Part of me wanted to be wanted. Besides, the Bible says we are to comfort the widow, the lonely, the needy and the hurting. My own family is well cared for. They don't need that much of my attention. And here's one who craves my presence, can't get along without me.

I said yes. Not once, but again, and again and again. I was hooked into a full-blown affair. I loved my mistress, and she returned that love to me. My family was not cut off. They were just "there". We had no animosity at home, just less and less involvement. My wife and I went from being lovers to being roommates.

My mistress and I had lots of exciting experiences together: picnics at the beach; long evenings of discussion; talks of the future for both of us. We even prayed together. In fact, we prayed together lots. That is one of the things that made the affair seem so right, so positive, and so acceptable. Our intimacies increased to the point where I felt for her every need, and she called me for every major decision. Our lives seemed to blend together in a warm bond of loving trust and mutual joy.

Then a cold splash of reality hit me like a bucket of ice

water. She is not my bride and never will be. She informed me that she belongs to someone else. I had to make some tough decisions. Caught between needing her attention and affection, and drawing on my own somewhat neglected marriage for those felt needs to be met, I felt like a fool.

I felt so vulnerable, so ashamed. So scared of admitting what had gone on. What would I tell my wife and my own children? How about, "Oh, hi there, family – I'm back. Sorry to have had an affair. Hope it didn't hurt you too much?" Or "Well, to tell you the truth, I just got caught up with my own ego needs and began to invest in the affair until there was nothing left for the family." Could my wife understand how the involvement had moved her out of my affection focus, yet I still loved her as my wife? Could I manage to overcome the affair and still have a marriage and family?

I didn't want it to be this way. It began with sincere devotion and paying attention to her needs (strange – it started with her needing me, and changed to me needing her). Then my love and affection began to produce results for her. It fed my ego. It seemed right, it felt so good! We were both so happy. But she began to pull me away from my own family responsibilities. I began to realize that sometimes I'd rather be with her than with my own wife and children. That is when I began to see the danger. The affair, I sensed, could destroy everything.

It is the affair that pastors do not want to face or talk about. *It is the affair with the church.*[1]

I have been there, done that, and got the T-shirt, but it's not a shirt I want to wear again. It is so subtle but so real. The work becomes all-consuming and families suffer along the way. We see it as being wholehearted for God, and so it may be, but the obsession it creates is hugely unhealthy if it is destructive of the lives closest to us.

I think back to when our boys were young. One simple

illustration will serve to make the point, but examples could be found in a whole variety of areas. It concerns the way the telephone would intrude on our lives. The phone is a very useful but exceedingly rude piece of equipment. You can be happily talking to someone and the phone rings. The person on the phone effectively says, "Stop what you are doing and talk to me." On many occasions I would be reading one of the boys a story at bedtime, enjoying my child, and the phone would ring. Off I would go and answer it, promising to be only a moment. What went through my son's mind? "Someone who is more important to my dad than I am has just interrupted our lives and he has put that person first."

That is what it must have felt like to my children. I could also mention the endless evenings I spent out, as well as a lack of family fun on Sundays. How many families have suffered because of the "affair of the church"? It's a hard balance to find, but we need to see our families, not as a barrier to God's work, but as a gift of God to us and a means of keeping us sane in the middle of that work, as well as being people who need our time and affection.

Rob Parsons, speaking to a group of financiers, said, "The days when your children want you to watch them in school plays, teach them to fly a kite, and listen to that story over and over again are very limited. The time is hurtling towards you when you're going to say to your fourteen-year-old, 'Do you fancy going fishing this weekend?' and he'll reply, 'Do you mind if we don't, Dad – I said I'd go out with some friends.'"

Parsons worked out that the number of days in the first 18 years of his children's lives is 6,575. "No amount of success can buy us one more day. If your child is ten years old, you have 2,922 left."

One businessman confided in him, "I've just been overseas for five days and when I got back I said to my fourteen-year-old boy, 'Well, have you missed me?' He said, 'No, Dad – because you're never here.'" The man went on, "You know what really upset me? It was that my son wasn't being sarcastic. He was just articulating what has for us become a lifestyle."

One practical way forward is to include in your diary family time, days out with the children, an evening a week for your spouse – quality time which is uninterrupted by church. In our present society, the diary has taken on a whole authority of its own. If someone asks you to do something and you look in your diary, don't be tempted to say, "Well, I'm free but I was planning to have time with my spouse this evening." It will appear to most people that you are in reality free and therefore available for whatever! If you fill your diary with "appointments" with your spouse and children, you can then look in your diary and say with great authority, "I am really sorry but I have an appointment this evening." Strangely enough, that will be totally acceptable to most people because of the incredible power of the "appointment in the diary"! So diary everything and you will feel wonderfully liberated and free of guilt because you have an "appointment".

You may think you can survive leadership if you don't put your family first but you will end your days with a great deal of regret as those closest to you are damaged by the pain you have caused.

Stop for a moment and consider:

1. How much has Christian ministry become my mistress?
2. What do I need to do today to change that?
3. What members of my family need an apology from me?

4. When will I begin to diary-in time for the family, not just for events, but "being" time?

5. How many evenings a week am I out on church business? If more than three, what am I going to do to change it?

6. How do I understand the emotional and relational needs of my family?

7. Do they think I put them first?

Notes

1. J. John & M. Stibbe, *A Box of Delights*, London, Monarch, 2001, pp.142–143.

Chapter 8

Run from the sexual snare

I cannot believe that it has happened again just as I sit down to write this. A friend has phoned to say his pastor has been found having an affair with a young member of staff. Is he repentant? Who knows? He was found out, so it is difficult to tell at this stage. Earlier this week I had lunch with a pastor friend. He shared with me how a mutual friend in ministry had just been discovered after having an affair lasting ten years! Over lunch another friend came up in conversation who, after years of preaching and teaching, had left his wife for a younger woman. Is this an epidemic or have I just picked a bad week? Who are these people?

They are just regular guys like you and me, and there "but for fortune" go any one of us, male or female. The tragic truth in all these situations is that everybody gets hurt. There are no winners. Spouses are emotionally torn apart, children bewildered, confused and let down, and the guilty party carries the scars for life. Moreover, the gospel is brought into disrepute yet again.

The discovery, from recent research, that large numbers of pastors and leaders struggle with internet pornography highlights the seriousness of the issues. The temptation to watch adult movies in the privacy of a hotel room is also a serious problem, not just for men in general, but also for male Christian leaders.

I believe that one of the problems that leads to this

situation is the loneliness and isolation of leaders. Responsibility breeds loneliness and loneliness is a breeding ground for a whole lot of unwanted offspring. We were not made to be alone. It is in the unnatural environment created by leadership that trouble comes. "Christendom Christianity" has produced a hierarchical view of leadership in the church, which isolates those at the top of the pile. It is very difficult to find our modern leadership structures in the New Testament, but we have grown up to believe that what we have is what was meant to be.

As I have got older, and particularly at the times when I have been unwell and forced to look at life in a fresh way, I have valued friendship more than anything else. How many people do you know of or have read about, who have become highly successful by the world's criteria, who have been there and done it all and are surrounded by the trappings of wealth, and yet end up miserable because they have no friends?

The sad fact is that the majority of men have almost no friends. They have colleagues, golf partners, and drinking buddies, but no real friends. It's also true that the majority of people in Christian leadership that I have come across have been unable to build friendships in church because of the strain it causes, and they don't make the time to get to know other people outside the church.

The pressures of church life can so easily be the cause of a growing lack of intimacy with spouse and family if we are not careful. When this happens, and it is usually a process over time, you are increasingly vulnerable. One of the reasons that leaders get depressed and drawn into sexual affairs, internet pornography and the like, is a lack of intimacy in human relationships.

Some years ago, a man fifteen years older than myself saw this potential problem in people in our position and got together six guys of my age to meet with him for 24 to 48 hours on a regular basis. We have now met three times a year for the last 24 years. These are men that I can be totally open with and who will ask me anything they want to. Our times together are both serious and challenging and also huge fun. They always include an overnight stay and good food and wine. These gatherings take priority over almost everything else in my life, but they are still not enough. Three times a year with close friends does not provide what is needed, although it is a huge help.

Women are more likely to have deep friendships than men, but it is not always the case. We all need two or three people that we can be real with, without fear of judgement, criticism or breaking confidence. We hear a lot today about the need for accountability but if you make yourself accountable outside of friendship, it rarely works. Why? Because what you want to do in secret, you will do whether you say you are accountable or not. Friends are more difficult to fool, but at the end of the day, it comes down to your own desire to stay free.

Some years ago, I went for breakfast with a friend who was staying in our city at a local hotel. During breakfast, a young lady who was also staying in the hotel and who was known to him came over to our table and he introduced me. Well, I was completely taken off guard by an immediate and very strong attraction to this woman. When I left the hotel, I knew I was in trouble, as I could not get her off my mind. I wanted to see her again but knew it would be destructive. Even so, I tried to find a way to justify another visit. The hold was so strong.

The only thing I knew to do was ring a friend. I shared my feelings with him, expecting him to empathize but not much else. "Well," he said, "what you need to do is to tell Lois about it." I wasn't at all sure that's what I wanted to do!

In the end I did just that and the strange thing was that the power of the attraction to the young woman waned almost right away. It took some time to fade but I knew I could never pursue it because my relationship with Lois was far too special to spoil. Nevertheless, I was frightened by the power of what happened and also by my potential to continue something secretly. I had needed a friend and he had said the right thing. Many are not so fortunate.

If loneliness is one issue, lack of self-discipline is another. The pressure of sexual temptation in the present climate is on us all (men and women) and Christians are not in any way exempt from this. Why should we be? We are sexual beings. A friend of mine who travels a lot will not even put on the TV in his hotel room to watch the news. He has made that decision to protect himself from temptation in an area where he knows he is vulnerable. It wouldn't be the case for everyone but it is for him. Another will never go to watch an 18-rated movie, even though many of them are good films. He knows his weakness. One group of leaders have set up the possibility of having regular computer checks by an expert who can discover what you have been looking at over the last period of time. Doing these sorts of things means you recognize your vulnerability and set up some protective boundaries.

Another issue is our relationship with God. A friend told me recently that he had said to his wife, "If ever I tell you that I love you more than I love God, watch out. It won't be long before I could love another woman more than you or God!" If you love God before anything or anyone else, you will not want to displease him in any way. You can be in full-time Christian leadership, preaching and teaching, and yet have lost your passion for God himself, particularly if the church has become your mistress. Make a note that a regular reading of the early chapters of Proverbs is always good medicine.

In all of this, it must be said that there is hope, even if you have failed. It is always going to be easier to receive forgiveness and healing if, when you have acted wrongly, you admit it and seek help. If you wait until you are found out, you are on a slippery slope to disaster. Because we all live with the same pressures, there should always be large quantities of understanding and grace.

You will never survive leadership if you do not face these sexual struggles in the company of trusted friends.

Stop for a moment and consider:

1. **At this moment, am I caught in a sexual trap?**
2. **Who will I go and talk to about it today, before it is too late?**
3. **What steps will I put in place to guard myself?**
4. **How much do I talk to my spouse about the pressures we both face?**

Chapter 9

Select the important over the urgent

Many people will have heard the story of the professor who stood before his class of students with a large empty jar and a pile of rocks, but it is well worth repeating. I have found it a huge help. He pointed to the pile of rocks and asked, "How many can I get in this jar?" After suggestions were made, he put as many stones into the jar as possible.

"Do you think the jar is now full?" he asked his students.

"Yes," they replied, as it was obvious that there was no space for more rocks. The professor took a pile of gravel and began to pour it in, shaking the jar as he did. The pieces of gravel settled in around the rocks. "Is it full now?" he asked. This time the students were unsure. He then took a bag of sand and poured it in until the jar looked full to capacity. At last the students were sure it was full but rather nervous to say so. The professor, smiling, took a jug of water and poured it into the jar. The water easily found room to settle. "That's it!" he announced proudly.

Then, he said, "Well, what is the point of this illustration?"

The reply came, "Well, there are gaps in life, and if you really work hard at it, you can always fit more in."

"No," he said, "the point is this: if you hadn't put the big rocks in first, you would never have got them in at all."

The important things are the big rocks. Many will have heard this illustration before but it is only when you start to put it into practice that you discover the incredible value of it. The principle really does work. But it takes discipline and courage to apply it.

The Christian ministry is filled with urgent demands. Everything feels like it must be done now, right away. And so often, the bigger, more important issues never get faced up to. Many years ago, Charles Hummell wrote a little booklet called "*The Tyranny of the Urgent*"[1], which had a profound effect on me. I found my own life so filled by things that had to be done *now* that I was failing to take a good hard look at the wider, more significant issues.

Hummell wrote, "The important tasks rarely must be done today or even this week. The urgent task calls for instant action...the momentary appeal of these tasks seem irresistible and important, and they devour our energy. But in the light of time's perspective, their deceptive prominence fades; with a sense of loss we recall the vital task we pushed aside. We realize we've become slaves to the tyranny of the urgent." We have to face the reality that for many, the urgent can be exhilarating. It can make you feel useful and important, and can bring instant gratification as you go around solving problems. It can easily provide a temporary high but the subsequent loss is not worth it.

Urgency in itself is not the problem. It is when it becomes so dominant that it pushes out everything else. It is then that the things that really need doing never get done. A member of our team came to me to apologize that he was never getting the things done that he really needed to accomplish. I couldn't figure out why this should be, so I asked him to write an event sheet of everything that happened during each day for one week. It made amazing and alarming reading both for him and me. About every five minutes of his day he was interrupted either by the phone, someone coming to his office needing something, or he was diverted by something else that came to his mind which he then went off and did. So we set some guidelines in place. For a certain period of time, all calls were diverted. A notice went on his door saying he was occupied but would be available at specific times. He also set himself a task list for each day. He was amazed at the change. When he'd done the big things, he still had space for many of the other things as well.

Of course the illustration of the jar and rocks has wider implications than just your working day. It asks the question, what are the important things in my life? Most of us will say that family and recreation are important to us, but our lives say something else. That's because when we begin with the immediate and the urgent, the things we really value are squeezed out.

Christian ministry and its pressures can be driven by real passion and commitment but it can get out of proportion. What are the "big rocks" in your life? Have you put them in place first or have they been squeezed out by a the plethora of noble and worthy causes that are actually not the main things? If you get your priorities right, there will be room for the rest. Get them wrong and they will never fit in, however hard you try.

The assumption, of course, is that if something is urgent it must be done first. It is very interesting that if you put on one side certain things that seem to say, "Urgent! Deal with me now! Do not delay or you will be in trouble", you may be surprised to discover that they were not that serious after all. In fact often, they either prove not to be as urgent as they appeared or they go away altogether.

It is amazing how some people who have needs that have been there for a very long time suddenly decide that if you do not see them right away, all will be lost. For most people, however, problems that took years to develop will almost certainly take time to deal with, and that process does not have to begin right now. A sociological study in which 50 people over the age of 95 were asked the question, "If you could have your life over again, what would you do differently?" produced some salutary responses. The most consistent answers were:

- I would reflect more;
- I would risk more;
- I would do more things that would live on after I die.

John Maxwell quotes the story of a young concert pianist who was asked the secret of her success. She replied, "Planned neglect". Then she explained, "When I was in school, there were many things that demanded my time. When I went to my room after breakfast, I made my bed, straightened the room, dusted the floor, and did whatever else came to my attention. Then I hurried to my piano practice. I found I wasn't progressing as I thought I should, so I reversed things. Until my practice period was completed, I deliberately neglected everything else. That programme of planned neglect, I believe, accounts for my success."

Maxwell also reveals why lion tamers use a four-legged stool. Apparently, the lion tries to focus on all four legs at the same time, causing a form of paralysis in the animal, and it becomes tame, weak and disabled. Maybe therein lies a lesson for all of us!

It is incredibly difficult to get this right but even seeing the potential of the problem is the first step in getting the better of it. We cannot survive leadership if we give all our time to the urgent. Not only will we be exhausted, but also the "big rocks" of our lives will never actually find a place. Decide now what those are and be ruthless in putting them in first position in your day or week.

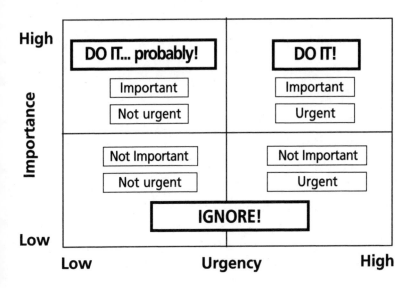

Stop for a moment and consider:

1. What are the big rocks in the wider perspective of my life?
2. What actually takes priority time, the important or the urgent?
3. What urgent things are shouting at me for attention today?
4. What more important things am I continually neglecting?

Notes

1. Charles Hummell, *The Tyranny of the Urgent,* Downers Grove, InterVarsity Press, 1994.

Chapter 10

Turn away from envy and be grateful

D o you sometimes wish your name was Bill Hybels or Rick Warren and you had a huge staff, a fabulous building, a stream of books to your name and people flocking to your conferences to listen to your words of wisdom and revel in your apparent success? Have you ever dreamed of being so well known that you are sought after by political leaders to give advice and say a prayer at key moments in your nation's history? Imagine having a stack of millionaires in your congregation, all wanting to put money into your ministry. Imagine being Billy Graham and speaking to vast crowds and seeing all those thousands come flocking forward to the front after your appeal.

And then you wake up and you're back to reality. Your building is in need of repair, the church council are blocking your latest idea and it seems a long time since anyone joined the church. You really wonder what you have achieved over so many years. This tendency to envy actually happens in all walks of life. We envy the rich and powerful, not the poor and downtrodden, but we rarely stop very long to consider what the pressures and heartaches are for such apparently privileged people.

I have often said to our congregation regarding material wealth, "Never look up with envy. Look down with thanksgiving." It is the natural tendency of human beings to look up to those who seem to have more, to be more successful, and to wish we could be like them. It speaks of a lack of contentment in having what we have and of an assumption that someone else's life is more fulfilled.

I imagine there are people who have looked at my situation with envy and I in turn have envied others. We have led a comparatively large church and I certainly am glad to be part of it, but it carries its own cost: increased responsibility; more people to keep an eye on and seek to help; and the potential for a huge amount of additional bureaucracy. There have been some days when I longed to go back to the simplicity of a church that could fit into a living room.

The book of Proverbs reminds us that,

> A heart at peace gives life to the body,
> But envy rots the bones. (Proverbs 14:30)

And also,

> Anger is cruel and fury overwhelming,
> But who can stand before jealousy? (Proverbs 27:4)

The apostle James wrote to the early church, "But if you harbour bitter envy and selfish ambition in your hearts, do not boast about it or deny the truth. Such 'wisdom' does not come down from heaven but is earthly, unspiritual, of the devil. For where you have envy and selfish ambition, there you find disorder and every evil practice" (James 3:14–16). Strong stuff!

In Andrew Roberts' book, *Hitler and Churchill*[1], he recalls Hitler's decision to revoke the orders of his Army High Command which, if carried out, would almost certainly have prevented the escape at Dunkirk. He overruled his generals purely because he could not allow them to get the glory. His envy of their better judgement destroyed his wisdom, which, in this case, mercifully meant deliverance for the allied forces. Hitler's ability as a leader was destroyed by his driving envy.

Envy is almost certainly one of the most destructive forces on planet earth and has caused the downfall of countless lives. It begins between children who want what another child has. It grows through adolescence with the desire for the clothes, possessions and friends that other people have. It continues through adulthood, eating destructively into the human heart. It is there in the hearts of countless leaders who hate to read of the success of others and cannot do so without a sideways thought of, "Why them and not me?"

If envy is not kept in check it will destroy your life and ministry. You will never survive if you allow it to get anywhere past the doorstep of your life. It needs to be the most unwelcome guest in your life because once it has taken up residence it will refuse to leave. It will create bitterness in your soul and lead you to behave in a way that will be destructive to you and others. I know, for I have felt its power, and its desire is never far away. But if there is one thing I have chosen to fight, it is envy, because I know its power and have felt its tentacles enveloping my mind.

I have been working and ministering in one city for over 33 years and although God has blessed us, there are things I have longed to do that have not happened. Over the years I have been privileged to lead a number of town-wide missions. Although these have been appreciated and relatively successful they have never been what I dreamed they could be. Recently, it was decided to invite an evangelist to our city, a man whom I have known and liked for many years. All the stops were pulled out and there was huge support, which was absolutely great. His events elsewhere have always pulled great crowds, far more than I have ever had. My immediate reaction to all of this was not to delight in what was happening through this evangelist, but to feel a sense of injustice that he should be so much more successful than me and that everyone was excited about him when I had been here all along. I felt the power of envy steal over me like a thick mist and sensed its desire to drag me down into a pit of depression. Thankfully I recognized it, as I have seen it before, and I knew I did not want to be overcome by its darkness.

The only way through envy is to own up to it, see it for the hideous thing that it is, and turn your heart to thankfulness. When I consider what I have seen, where I have been, what I have done, how I have been blessed, I am overwhelmed with gratitude. When I look at so much of the world struggling in poverty, ill health and darkness, I cannot believe how fortunate I am and have been. When I look at this man's ministry, I am so delighted that he is being so used and desire the very best for him and our city. How can I really be anything but grateful? It is in turning to positive expressions of thankfulness that I break the power of the evil of envy.

If envy creeps in, it forces you to take your eye off the ball and on to someone else's game. Not only do you end up with a hard heart but you also lose sight of the value of what you are called and gifted to be and do. God will hold us all responsible and accountable for what we did with what we were given. We will not be accountable for anyone else. We are required to take hold of the gifts and talents *we* were given, in the place *we* were assigned, at *our* time in history and to be faithful. It is God who opens and closes doors. He makes room for our gifts. He not only gifts us but places us in the sphere in which those gifts are to operate.

Years ago, I remember having a meal with a friend and colleague. We had been working together for some time. I was happily married and he was single. We both were feeling a bit down and I asked what was bothering him. He said that he envied me being married and having someone to go home to each day. When he asked me what was on my mind, I had to laugh. "I was just thinking how lucky you are to be free to come and go as you please with no one else to have to think about!" It was not a reflection on my marriage or even his singleness, but we both saw things in each other's lives that we envied. We cannot live that way and be free.

Real freedom comes through gratitude. Brennan Manning writes in his excellent book, *Ruthless Trust*,

> Let's say that I interview ten people, asking them the same question – "Do you trust God?" – and each one answered, "yes, I trust God," but nine out of ten actually did not trust Him. How would I find out which of these ragamuffins was telling the truth? I would videotape each of the ten lives for a month and then, after watching the videos, pass judgement using this criterion: the person with an abiding spirit of gratitude is the one who trusts God. The foremost quality of a trusting disciple is gratefulness. Gratitude arises from the lived perception, evaluation, and acceptance of all of life as grace – as an undeserved and unearned gift from the Father's hand.[2]

Henri Nouwen wrote,

> To be grateful for the good things that happen to us in our lives is easy, but to be grateful for all our lives – the good as well as the bad, moments of joy as well as moments of sorrow, the successes as well as the failures, the rewards as well as the rejections – that requires hard spiritual work. Still, we are only grateful people when we can say thank you to all that has brought us to the present moment. Let's not be afraid to look at everything that has brought us to where we are now and trust that we will soon see in it the guiding hand of a loving God.

Deal with the thoughts that lead to envy as fast as you can or you will never survive leadership. You and I will never survive without the spirit of gratitude filling every part of our lives. It is the secret of freedom and joy that nothing can take away.

Stop for a moment and consider:

1. **Whom do I envy and why? Pray for a blessing on that person.**
2. **How has envy sought to get a hold on my life?**
3. **Take a piece of paper today and list all the things for which you are grateful.**

Notes

1. Andrew Roberts, *Hitler and Churchill,* London, Phoenix House, 2004.
2. Brennan Manning, *Ruthless Trust,* San Francisco, HarperCollins, 2002.

Chapter 11

Forgive ruthlessly

C.S. Lewis once said that everyone believes forgiveness is a good idea until they have to forgive someone. This is very relevant to preachers, who often speak on the great themes of forgiveness and reconciliation but find it difficult when they themselves have been hurt.

To be in Christian leadership is actually a recipe for being hurt. Anyone who has been in leadership for any time and denies any sense of hurt is either lying or dead! If you're attempting to work at any level with people, then it is not possible to avoid hurt or pain. We hurt others and get hurt by them. I have hurt scores of people over the years, as far as I am aware none of them deliberately. The most common cause is false expectations. Someone has an expectation of me towards them, but never actually tells me what it is. Or even if they do, I fail to live up to their expectations and let them down. As a result, some people have held resentment for years while I was totally unaware of what was going on. I have "said things", "not said things", "done things" and "not done things" that have upset people. I know that this has happened because people have told me, often years later.

Life is a minefield and it is impossible not to be hurt at some stage. It goes with the job. People behave badly. Some intend to cause pain but most don't. They just don't understand what they are doing. And when enough hurts build up, it's easy to fall apart under the sheer weariness of it. People will do things and say things that hurt and you, as the leader, will often be the first to be blamed.

In football, when a team plays badly, critics do not put the blame primarily on the players but on the manager. He is not even on the pitch and yet his job is on the line if they go on losing games. So it is with leadership. You may or may not get praised when things go right but you are very likely to be blamed when they don't!

The deepest hurts that I have felt have come from people that I cared about. I have felt betrayed by close friends, publicly challenged and put on the spot by people who should have cared about how I felt. I have been harshly blamed for other people's mistakes, criticized for my views and written about unfairly, but that is no more than the lot of most leaders! And it hurts!

A bishop in the Church of England told me that he had a call from one of the local vicars in his diocese, saying he had had several very negative letters from church members in the previous months. He told me his reply was, "In my experience that is pretty normal. I wouldn't worry until you get several a week, then get in touch with me again!"

In the course of my years in ministry, I have been hurt by a number of people, some very close. It is difficult to write in detail about them here because many of the people concerned are still alive and I would, without a doubt, only share from my perspective, and my perspective on events is only half the story. It is my perception of those things, though, that causes the damage and that is what I have to deal with. In many cases I doubt these people had any malicious intent or understood how deep the wound was. All I can be sure of is that I know what anger and resentment feel like. I have often felt like quitting on the basis that it just wasn't worth the pain. I have sat and listened to scores of leaders tell of how they have been abused, mistreated and insulted by elders, deacons, members of parish church councils and the like. Often this is at the hands of those who are in places of authority at work and who think they then have the right to throw their weight around in the church as well.

(As an aside, let me say that I have learnt a very important principle and it is this: never write a letter saying something negative to a person. Speak to the individual's face. Always write a letter of praise and thankfulness. Why? Because people keep letters and they can keep going over them for years to come. It takes at least ten good letters to overcome the effects of one bad one. So try not to cause that problem for others.)

You cannot possibly stay in the place of hurt and self-pity if you want to survive. And that is where forgiveness comes in, which is at times so very hard. Vengeance is the easy option. The only way to survive and the only way to stay free is to forgive, and you need to, because it is the Jesus way.

I have often spoken on forgiveness but I am increasingly coming to terms with what it fully means. It means that I no longer want the person who has hurt me to receive some sort of punishment for what they have done. It is about letting God sort it out. It is coming to terms with pain as well as understanding the mind of the offender. I need to face the reality that someone else's words or actions have caused me pain and take ownership of it. The pain is very real and I cannot afford to minimize the effect on my life. It is quite possible, though, that the offender had little idea of the offence and pain they were causing. Understanding that, I then choose whether I will wallow in the thoughts of how badly I have been treated or get up and move on. It begins with an act of the will: a willingness to release the person from my judgement and my right to vengeance. The sense of emotional release often comes later.

It is also a process. How often have you thought you had

forgiven and then, faced with the person again, all the same anger and hurt rises up? I believe that even though forgiveness can begin right away, human pain is never removed quickly. Deep scars take time to heal. With one individual I found that every time I met him, I felt the anger rise, and I had to learn to look at him and in my mind say, "I forgive you. I release you from my judgement." Each time I did that, the reaction was less, until eventually it was gone. If you were to ask me whether I would trust that person again in the same situation, the answer is probably, "No, I wouldn't." But then I don't think that I am required by God to be gullible and foolish. Trust is a very different issue from forgiveness. I want to know every day that I could look any person in the eyes with a clear conscience and a sense that "all is well between us". I believe that to be the case and it feels good.

I think that it is true that many (but not all) people who leave a church for any reason other than a geographical move, leave because of hurt. But it is often difficult if they hide behind the reason – "The Lord has told me to go [to wherever]" – which is usually sheer avoidance of facing up to their own responsibility. After all, who can argue with the Lord himself? Sometimes the move is immediate but very often it isn't. More often from the point of hurt, people disengage and then leave at a later stage. We do not deal with hurt well. The tragedy is that if we don't, we take it with us. It is compounded the next time it happens.

I say this because many leaders also leave a place with unresolved hurt in their hearts. They move on to start over somewhere else but the ache is always there until it is dealt with. Whether leader or people, all of this can lead to physical sickness later in life. It really isn't worth the sense of self-righteousness and deep anger if you end up sick in mind and body.

In some (but by no means all) situations, in order to get clear, you will need to go to the people concerned, confess your pain and resentment, and give them the chance to be reconciled. That is not always possible and should never be done if it only provides an opportunity for more blame to be meted out, but many times it enables the situation to end well, with the various parties at peace.

I think it helps to go beyond forgiveness into blessing people and that is the way to experience freedom. I once suggested to our church that they should give Christmas presents to people who had hurt them. This idea proved a mistake as some people received unexpected gifts and immediately wondered what they had done to hurt the giver! But generally it is a good principle to find a way to bless those who hurt you. It will bring surprising results and great joy.

I headed this section "Forgive ruthlessly" because nothing except ruthless forgiving will do. We have to keep short accounts and you cannot let anything go under the carpet under the guise that "it was nothing really". It is always something, and if a hurt is allowed to fester it will come back to cause more trouble later on. In the marriage relationship, we are told not to let the sun go down on our anger. That means getting right with each other on a daily basis. In other relationships, you can try to avoid the issue but in reality it never goes away. It may well prove a great help to have a buddy that you share pain with. He or she can encourage you in sorting things out.

Most of us will lead others through a process of forgiveness for past hurts that go back to early family life when so much damage can be done by words, actions and neglect from parents. It is all too easy to bring this insight to others and neglect it in ourselves. It is amazing how many of these early bad experiences start to do their real damage at middle age.

Maybe because we live such hectic lives up till then, we can cover over the cracks. Is it possible that many pastors get into difficulties in middle years because they themselves have never dealt with their own deep issues? It may be that many more in leadership should receive counselling themselves. It would also serve us all well to have people to whom we could go for a regular "MOT" inspection of our lives. Remember, we too are fellow travellers with everyone else. We are made of the same stuff and experience the same traumas. We too need help and nurture.

All of this sounds straightforward as I write it, but I know it isn't. C.S. Lewis is right: forgiveness is a good idea until you have to do it. It may be hard but it will undoubtedly save your life.

You cannot survive leadership without ruthlessly forgiving.

Stop for a moment and consider:

1. **Where am I still hurting and from what?**
2. **What person am I going to share with to help me to a place of forgiveness and release?**
3. **What will I do today to begin this process?**
4. **Whom do I need to bless as a sign of forgiveness?**

Chapter 12

Maintain your devotional life

I t seems so strange to be reminding pastors and leaders of the need to maintain a personal devotional life. Of all people, we should have no difficulty in this area. Yet I have to confess that it has been for me a continual struggle. If this is no problem to you, then skip this chapter, but only do so if you are being honest. Let me make it clear: I am not talking about Bible study, wrestling with a text and thinking through its meaning for the main purpose of preparing to deliver a sermon. I am not talking about crying out to God in times of desperation because you do not know what to do or say in a church crisis. I am talking about unhurried, no-agenda, quality time spent with God and his Word, just for you and nobody else, and on a regular basis. For the "busy" leader, however, this becomes surprisingly difficult.

May I suggest a few keys?

A discipline

I really do not want to lay some legalistic burden on everyone, which just leaves us all feeling guilty, as this is all about a relationship not a duty. But I have observed that the natural pattern for our lives is only to do things that we are going to enjoy; in other words whatever is a "delight" to us. Sometimes we will do things because we are overcome by a sudden desire for something. If we carry out Christian disciplines like giving, fasting or prayer on the basis of desire or delight, we will only rarely participate. But if we begin with discipline, the outcome is radically changed. What begins in discipline may well then become desire and then delight.

Daniel, it would seem, survived the pressures of Babylon because he had created a discipline of prayer in his life. We are told that "Three times a day, he got down on his knees and prayed, giving thanks to his God, just as he had done before" (Daniel 6:10). This practice was for him a discipline, a habit and often a joy as it was filled with gratitude and thanksgiving. It was also a necessity. It kept him close to the God he served in the midst of an alien environment.

I don't think we should beat ourselves over the head when we miss times like these, but to have a pattern in life is hugely helpful. Our walk with God is not a religious duty. It is a relationship. But all worthwhile relationships need some discipline to maintain them well.

We do not do this because we are leaders or pastors, but because we are God's children. However, if we are to minister to others, we especially need to come from being in a good place with the Lord. We must come from the place of closeness to him if we are to bring his Word to others.

A place

If you have your personal times with God in the same place that you prepare sermons, you will easily slip into "sermon mode".

At a conference for headteachers, the lecturer, a very experienced former head, was encouraging his listeners to have a "thinking chair". This would be a chair in their office that would only be sat in for times of no-agenda thinking. When they sat in the chair, it was not to do any work or regular reading. Their minds were to associate this chair with one thing only: freedom to think.

In the same way, to have a place, a chair even, that is set aside for your devotional time may force you out of the sermon mode where you tend to think, "This will do for someone else", and may instead become a place of sanctuary for you and God. Many like to walk and pray; some prefer to sit and be quiet. Whatever suits you is best, as long as it is special.

An aid

I have been hugely indebted to the people who put together the *The One Year Bible (Tyndale Press)*. It has been such a help to me and given me a discipline and framework for daily reading. Some use a lectionary; others have a variety of aids. Either way, to have something to regulate your reading is such a help. Many find it helpful to have a notebook and pen to hand, to write down thoughts as they come. Some people I know have testified to the value of journaling. I have only done this in fits and starts but I can see the huge value of it. It requires discipline and application but it is wonderful to be able to look back and track your journey.

A retreat

It is interesting that Jesus put "away" times into the schedule with the disciples. Some were times when he went alone to pray; others were "come aside and rest awhile" times. I think we need both. Because life is full (and especially if you have a young family or other dependents), it is difficult to get all the time you want and therefore time away to "retreat" is a huge benefit. This might be for a day or even longer. It could be a walk in the country or something more structured at a retreat centre. Whichever it is, to get away several times a year, on your own, to reflect and take stock, will reap huge rewards. This is not the same as a day off, which is an essential part of life but is often taken up with family things. I wish I had been disciplined enough to put retreats into my diary much earlier in my ministry. I would have been far more relaxed and refreshed. It would have put some breaks into the system. In the UK we have notices on the motorways that say, "Tiredness kills. Take a break!" We retreat not just to overcome tiredness but to keep our souls in touch with the One in whose hands we have placed our lives.

A warning

I don't think any of this is easy but I do think it is fruitful! If you are naturally an A-type personality, standing still is difficult at any time. If you have an active family or needy dependents, finding time is difficult. Those of our congregations in "normal" employment have to find time in their busy day, so it should be possible for us. If we haven't worked out the reality of it then we won't be much help to anyone else. The important thing is that the Christian life is a walk and we must learn to know God's presence day by day wherever we are.

We neglect this at our peril. I cannot see how we can hope to survive church leadership without a devotional life of prayer and the Word. I would urge you, if this is an area in which you have struggled, to take stock and put some disciplines into your life.

Stop for a moment and consider:

1. What is the state of my devotional life?
2. What gets in the way of my times of quiet with God?
3. What can I do to be more disciplined?
4. What retreats have I planned for the coming year?
5. Where will I choose as my devotional place?

Chapter 13

Avoid the pressure of the latest thing

If there is one thing that brings a sinking feeling to the heart of a pastor it is the excited words of a well-meaning church member, "Have you heard what God is doing in...? I think we had better go and see what they're doing. In fact, there are trips being planned to visit there and some of us are planning to go and see and bring back what we can. I know you'll be pleased!"

Globalization is both a blessing and a curse. On the one hand, it gives us a great sense of being part of one world and one church. We can almost immediately feel an affinity with the suffering and the joys of other people. Wherever we go (and nowadays, there is hardly any limit to where anyone can go), we do not need to feel cut off from friends and family. Modern communication through phone, fax and email has transformed our ability to keep in touch with an extraordinary sense of immediacy. Television brings every part of the globe into our living room. Air travel means that almost nowhere is more than a day away. What a contrast to only a century ago! Because of this, we can also benefit from the thoughts, ideas and vision of the worldwide church and feel closeness with brothers and sisters everywhere. We no longer need to be enclosed by the smallness of our own situation. But there is another side to the coin.

We are now exposed to teaching, ideas, programmes and methods from every corner of the globe. What God does uniquely in one place, with one culture, at one point in time, becomes universal knowledge. If it is accompanied by the trappings of what is considered success (and that is nearly always related to numbers), then it becomes a huge attraction to go and see, get the package, and bring it back. The truth is that many crave "success" so much, for good or poor motives, that when they hear of something "successful" elsewhere, it is almost impossible not to want it for themselves. The wonderful possibility of "immediate success" becomes a huge carrot in front of us or a huge pressure put on us by other well-meaning people. We ourselves may not be drawn to it, but members of our congregation who have their ears attuned to the latest thing will come knocking on our door. How can we refuse if we don't want to appear unspiritual? And it must be said that many will be blessed by their encounters with other places. This section is not a denial of that fact.

In the last few years, thousands of bounty-seeking pastors have left Britain for Korea, Singapore, Chicago, Argentina, Toronto, Pensacola, and at the time of writing, Orange County and Bogotá seem to be the places to go! Of course by the time you read this, there may well be another hot spot on the Christian map beckoning us to taste its wares, conferences, tapes, DVDs, T-shirts and the rest (or more likely wishing we would all stay away and let them get on with what God has uniquely and sovereignly called them to do). Some or all of these places may be areas of wonderful blessing from God, uniquely fashioned for the people in that place and time. But tapes and videos get passed around, and men and women in ministry criss-cross the globe telling their particular story.

Where do poor local pastors fit into this scenario? They are trying to find God's way for their own situation and seeking to be faithful to what they and their team feel called to do. They may have tried one of the recent ideas and just as they are getting going in that, they hear from other leaders or members of their congregation, "Pastor, have you heard about...?", the implication being that this is where the action is and if you don't get in on it you could well miss out on all God has for you. The pressure of the latest "wave" can be incredibly strong. No one wants to miss out and many feel they are only one secret key away from breakthrough!

We are generally not good at seeing principles as opposed to methods. If we were, we would spot the underlying principle that has worked and stay with that, and we would save ourselves a great deal of heartache.

Now I know there may be a cry of objection at this point from those who have been blessed and helped by something imported from outside. If that is true for you then great! But be careful that when that wave dies down you aren't out again eagerly searching for the latest fad. You may not kill yourself but you may well destroy the church.

It requires courage to steer a straight path, to set out in a particular direction and not be detoured along the way. I like the title of one of Eugene Peterson's books, *A Long Obedience in the Same Direction*[1]. It summarizes what the Christian life is all about and ultimately what church life is all about. The churches you and I rush around the world to copy were doing just that: being obedient. All the places on the pilgrimage map are "first copies". These congregations found something by pursuing a given course under the guidance of God as best they knew, and at some point breakthrough came.

If you are doing something "because it works in Bogotá", for example, then you had better be sure you understand why it works well there, the cultural influences, the background, and the national context. There may well be principles to be followed but beware of copying the method.

I am in no way trying to discourage us from taking risks, being innovative or reaching for new things, but the pressure of the latest wave can be very strong. It takes huge courage to keep your eyes ahead and keep going on the path you have set. My own observation is that the less faddish a church is, the better it does in the long term. Novelty may bring short-term gains but will fail in the long haul. And we want to be in it for the long haul.

It can sometimes be helpful to gain from the insights of the business world. Whether we are in business or church, we are all trying to move in a given direction with a group of people with a specific goal in mind (and if it works well, it is probably a godly principle anyway).

Jim Collins, in his excellent book, *Good to Great*[2], studies eleven companies that were good companies but became great ones. He found a number of principles that were common to all. One interesting finding was this: there was no great new idea or scheme that changed everything. There was no "trumpet-blowing start day" for a new idea. The company may have embraced new ways of doing things but these were slowly integrated rather than being "the answer to the problem". In fact, it was difficult to know what made the change from good to great. It just happened as the companies faithfully pursued their target. Those businesses that were continually coming up with "the latest new idea" always failed in the long run. They could not sustain it.

Collins likens the process to turning a huge flywheel which is very difficult and very slow to move at first, but which slowly begins to turn. Then at some point – breakthrough! For the same amount of work, the "wheel" goes faster and faster. And nobody knows when or why the breakthrough comes. He writes, "There was no single defining action, no grand programme, no one killer innovation, no solitary lucky break... it comes about by a cumulative process – step by step, action by action, decision by decision."

Another principle that I found very interesting was what he called the "Stockdale principle". It was named after Admiral Jim Stockdale, a high-ranking USA officer taken captive during the Vietnam War. He managed to survive and was the source of inspiration that enabled many other men to make it through. Jim Collins recalls the following conversation with him: "I asked, 'Who didn't make it out?' 'Oh, that's easy,' he said. 'The optimists. They are the ones who said that they were going to be out by Christmas. And Christmas would come and go and they'd say, "We are going to be out by Easter." They died of a broken heart.'"

He wasn't saying that it is better to be a pessimist than an optimist, but that the suggestion that a new idea will provide a quick fix and sort everything out is almost always unreal and dangerous in the long term. Those who "confront the brutal facts of their reality and believe they will prevail in the end are still standing at the end of the day". Continuing with the "right things" and being prepared for the long haul will get you there in the end. You will create an atmosphere of hope but also of perseverance.

The promises of revival and therefore the desperation to find the key to bring it about have done us few favours. In fact, they leave the church with a continual sense of disappointment instead of determination to press on, whatever should come about. Don't give in to the pressure of the latest fad. Rejoice in another's blessing but don't let it cause you to stray from the path assigned to you.

If you want to survive leadership, you need to set a clear course. Be open to new principles but do not be led off course by the latest fad moving across the Christian horizon, even if it is proving to be a great blessing elsewhere.

Stop for a moment and consider:

1. When have I confused method with principle?
2. What pressure am I under at this present time to take something new on board?
3. How am I dealing with this pressure to "not miss it"?
4. How am I seeking God's way that is particular to me and my congregation?

Notes

1. Eugene Peterson, *A Long Obedience in the Same Direction*, Leicester, IVP, 2000.
2. Jim Collins, *Good to Great*, London, Random House Business Books, 2001.

Chapter 14

Prioritize the right people

This principle is important in two key areas for every leader. It is important with regard to the people in the church that we care for, and also the people we work with. The first, whom we have not chosen, will, by the nature of the work, be people we are trying to help. These, to a greater or lesser degree, require time and energy. The second we can choose and the wrong choice can be damaging to our health and well-being.

Firstly, let's consider the church members. If you look at the diary of most pastors, it will quickly become obvious that a large amount of time is taken up with "needy people", of which there are at least two sorts. There are ordinary folk who from time to time get into a mess and have a crisis. They don't want to take up your time; in fact, they feel bad about bothering you. Many even feel they are being a nuisance. Spending time with people like this is part and parcel of what the pastoral ministry is all about. It is a privilege to help them be repaired so that they can enter fully into normal life and activity again. Most of us fall into this group at some point in our lives and we are glad to have people around to help and support us.

The other group of "needy people", on the whole, do *not* feel bad about bothering you (after all, that is what you are there for and paid to do!). They will usually have to see you right away and on a regular basis. What marks these people out is that they rarely get any better. You can counsel them with the greatest techniques known to pastors. You can cast everything out that you can possibly imagine. You can care till you are blue in the face – and nothing really changes. These are the people that Carl George refers to, in his book on small groups[1], as EGRs. They are "extra grace required people".

I remember somebody once telling me that the best job in the world is to be a consultant dermatologist in a private practice. The patients pay high fees for a consultation but never fully recover, so you have an income for life. (If you are a dermatologist please forgive this gross exaggeration.) Unfortunately it doesn't work like that in the ministry. These "EGR" people will eventually drain every drop of enthusiasm you have because you will feel obliged to see them and feel extremely guilty if you do not.

I used to feel envious of people with large churches until ours became quite large and I realized that you collect difficult people in proportion to your size. Now, I want to make it clear, I am in no way maligning those people. They are indeed people with serious need but you had better be very careful that a caring heart does not lead you into a trap which will eventually make you ineffective for the task God has called you to. You need to find a way to deal with it. I would suggest you provide limited regular time for these people and you spread them out to a number of others who can share the load. You may, in fact, not be the best person to deal with their need anyway. Sometimes people will play on your need for significance by demanding to see "the leader" because no one else will do.

These people come into the category of the "urgent". They will normally say they only want "ten minutes" but they really want hours. The others are the "important", because often they are "wounded soldiers". When they are helped and healed they will be back in service. Distinguishing between the two takes wisdom. Not distinguishing may cause burnout.

So often, the majority of time is allocated to those in need as opposed to those who appear OK. Because needy people "need" you, it is easy to forget those that seem fine. The people who are serving and giving their lives in a meaningful way are abandoned until there is a crisis. Shouldn't it be the other way around? The majority of time should be given to encouraging the healthy so they don't get sick. It is the "good" people who should be getting our quality time so that they can be even more effective in what they are doing.

One small bit of encouragement goes a long way to keep someone on the road. I have often heard people say, "The pastor never takes an interest in me unless I am sick." We can easily feel guilty spending time with the well but that is partly what Jesus did. He put clear boundaries around his public ministry, and a good part of his time was given to the disciples because in the long term they themselves would minister to the sick. When the apostles in the early days of the church saw their time being wrongly used, they gave themselves to ministry to the believers, who in turn helped the poor and needy.

Secondly, with regard to the people you work closely with in leadership, you can know whether you have the right people by the effect they have on you. People who come into your office will create one of two different effects. Some will walk out leaving you sad that they are going because their visit has done you good. When you know they are coming to see you for whatever reason, your heart is lifted. There are others that have the opposite effect. When they leave, you feel rather relieved because their visit has left you drained. In future when you look in your diary and see they are due a visit, you begin to dread it.

A friend who is a teacher made this comment to me, "One

of the reasons that I'm often a little late home is that at the end of the day, I will pop in and see the headteacher about something and he just seems to want to chat. In fact he offloads some stuff from his day. He doesn't expect me to do anything except listen, but I'm amazed how often I get delayed just talking with him." The reason is that for the headteacher, this friend of mine is the sort of person whose company makes you feel good. If you fill your life with a higher proportion of "drainers" you will be continually drained. If you spend time with "givers" you will find yourself energized.

In his brilliant book, *Courageous Leadership*[2], Bill Hybels cites three key characteristics for picking people to work with you. He says that character, competence and chemistry are the essentials. We would normally settle for character and competence and not worry too much about the third. He recalls a conversation with Ken Blanchard, co-author of *The One Minute Manager*[3], who counselled him never to invite a person onto his team who did not have a positive effect on him the minute he or she walked into his office. Many people reading this will almost certainly realize that that isn't true for them. As a result, they find themselves drained by their relationships and life is a struggle.

However important competence may be, and it is obviously essential, if it is not matched by chemistry, life with these people will always be a drain on you. I do not think you can survive in leadership very long if you do not have people around you who are life-giving. A friend of mine runs a very successful and profitable company. It is not difficult to work out why it has done so well. Not only is he an extremely gifted leader but he has also surrounded himself with people he likes. In fact, a group of young men started out with him and are still around, 30 years later. They have grown up together and respect one another. The same is true of the Billy Graham organization. The secret of their success is not just the huge giftedness of Billy Graham as a preacher and communicator but also the fact that he is still, at the time of writing, working with much the same team he had at the beginning. They have grown old together. This could never have happened if they did not find each other life-giving and enjoyable to work with.

Work can be fun when you do it with the right people. It can be tiring, discouraging and draining if you are doing it with the wrong people for you. Many Christian leaders are tired and worn out because so much of their time has been spent with those who are draining the system, and they are working with people who are not much fun to be with. You can survive that way for a short time but not in the long term.

We may be worn out in well-doing because we have focussed too much on the wrong people. You cannot survive leadership in the long term by doing that.

Stop for a moment and consider:

1. How much time do I give to those who drain me?
2. What helpful boundaries could I put in place?
3. How could I spread the load?
4. Who, in my team, full-time or not, energizes me, and who drains me?
5. How much time do I give to those who are "well" who need encouragement from me to do even better?

Notes

1. Carl George, *Prepare Your Church for the Future*, Grand Rapids, Revell, 1991.
2. Bill Hybels, *Courageous Leadership*, Grand Rapids, Zondervan, 2002.
3. Kenneth Blanchard, *The One Minute Manager*, New York, Berkley Trade, 1983.

Chapter 15

See your life in perspective

There are times when I have behaved as if, when I die, God will say to himself, "Is there any point in going on with life on earth any more? Nick is no longer there, so probably nothing of any significance will ever happen again. Nothing of real value happened before he arrived and nothing will happen from now on. What a pity he could not have achieved even more! If he had worked harder, gone to more meetings and taken on a few more projects there is no telling where the world would be!"

There are other times in my life where I have felt that my short life on earth was of no consequence whatsoever. There was really no point in doing anything because what did it matter anyway? Life will go on. The world will not stop and who cares at the end of the day? When I go, it will be like a man taking his hand out of a bucket of water. The water will immediately close in on the gap as if the hand had never been there.

Neither of these attitudes is healthy or true. We live the early part of our lives with huge dreams of what can be achieved and when we get to 40-plus we begin to realize that so much we hoped for will never happen. What began in great expectation can end in disappointment, until we see our lives in the perspective of God's work in human history. It is good to find that Solomon struggled with the same issues of meaning and meaninglessness when he wrote the book of Ecclesiastes.

We are part of history. We are baton carriers in a relay race. The people before us ran as best as they could, but their lives were not the whole thing. We are to run in our moment of history, using our gifts, talents, opportunities and relationships to do the best we can. When we finally run out of breath, others will come after us and continue the race.

We are living in the legacy of previous generations but we are also building something which future generations will either benefit from or have to cope with (probably a mixture of both). In the area of the global environment, it is very easy to feel that we can do nothing and anyway we won't be here when it really gets bad. Being fully human, however, means preparing for the future in a way you wish others had done for you.

I have lived and worked in the same city for many years. We have seen tremendous changes in that time. So many great things have happened, and it would be easy for me to think that all the real action has happened here since 1972! The truth is that we have only done what we have done because of the work of those who came before us. When I hear newcomers to the city talking as if there were no history before them, I feel like shouting, "Let me tell you about the things that went on before you came. You are building on a great history!"

The Bible has a fantastic thing to say about King David. It says, "David... served God's purpose in his own generation, [then] he fell asleep" (Acts 13:36). That is all that needs to be written about us. "Nick served the Lord in his generation and then fell asleep!" That will do me fine.

Jesus lived his life in perspective. Out of a life of 33 years, he was only in the public eye for three years. He did not seem to think it necessary to do all the things that we deem essential to have a successful ministry. He knew what he had come to do and did it. He did not need to go to the Gentiles, he never went to Rome, and he did not plant churches everywhere or start an organization. He knew that would be done by others and was happy for it to be so. His life was in perspective. He knew he was on time. He knew what had gone before. He knew what would come next and was secure enough to do what he uniquely could do and then leave. It is quite a thing that after the resurrection, he did not stay longer. The potential was huge for a resurrected man! In fact, there would have been no limits to what he could have done. But there would have been no church, no releasing of the vast array of gifts and ministries that were to come in others. Jesus saw his life in perspective.

What has this got to do with surviving leadership? Everything! There will be many dreams and longings we have that will never be experienced in our lifetime. It doesn't mean they aren't God-given but it may mean they are not for us. David never personally built the Temple even though he longed to see a "dwelling place for God". If you get your life out of perspective, you will kill yourself trying to achieve what you were never meant to do. Of course, you need to live with passion and seek to be everything you were made to be. Athletes maintain momentum until the end of the race (or their part of it) by aiming at a point beyond their finishing line so they do not drop off speed at the last minute. Many of the dreams we have, and the things God has put in our hearts, are beyond the tape, but our desire to see them fulfilled will keep us in the race until the end.

Seeing your life in the perspective of history will have two other effects. Firstly, it will help you to appreciate the past and all that others have done. You will find you want to discover the history of where you are and those who carried the torch before you. When I was at school my teacher said to me, "I think you are about the worst pupil at history I have ever taught!" This remark was not helpful! I assumed from there on that history and I would never get on. In my later years, however, I have begun to take a far greater interest in history, in order to see my own time in perspective.

Secondly, it will make you think more about what you pass on. Some want only to leave memorials to themselves and their great achievements. Others, who see their lives in perspective, want to leave in a way that enables others to build on what has gone before and if possible to go on to greater things. You need to find yourself shouting to a younger generation, "Run the race as best you can and win the prize!"

St Paul ended his life with the words, "I have fought the good fight, I have finished the race, I have kept the faith. Now there is in store for me the crown of righteousness..." (2 Timothy 4:7–8). The perspective of his life was related to what was yet ahead. He saw this life as important but only as the overture before the main event. This is not "it". It is the preparation for "it". What we do now prepares us for eternity. It all seems so important now, but in the light of the future it is very small. When your life and work is put in the light of all that is to come, however valuable it has been, it will only be a preparation.

Sometimes we need to say to ourselves, "Get real. Lighten up. You have everything out of perspective in the light of the whole picture." The picture includes the past. It includes the future on earth but it is set against the backdrop of eternity. In that context, the missed meeting, the bad sermon, the failed church plant and the terrible deacons meeting do not really matter.

You will never survive leadership by believing it all hangs and falls on you. Get your life into the perspective of Heaven and of eternity. Realize that your part is essential to the whole but it is not *the* whole.

Here are the "reflections" of Oscar Romero, Archbishop of El Salvador, who gave his life defending the poor. I hope his thoughts will touch and encourage you.

It helps now and then to step back
and take the long view.
The reign of God is not only beyond our efforts,
It is even beyond our vision

We accomplish in our lifetime
only a tiny fraction of the magnificent enterprise
that is God's work.
Nothing we do is complete
which is another way of saying
that the reign of God lies beyond us.
No statement says all that can be said.
No prayer fully expresses our faith.
No confession brings perfection.
No pastoral visit brings wholeness.
No programme accomplishes our mission.
No set of goals and objectives includes everything.

This is what we are about.
We plant seeds that someday will grow.
We water seeds already planted,
knowing that they hold future promise.
We lay foundations that will need further development.
We provide yeast that produces effects
far beyond our capabilities.

We cannot do everything
and there is a sense of liberation in realizing that.
This enables us to do something and do it well.
It may be incomplete, a step along the way,
an opportunity for God's grace to enter and do the rest.

We may never see the end result of our efforts.
We are prophets of a future not our own.[1]

Stop for a moment and consider:

1. How would my life change if it were lived in perspective?
2. What am I aiming at that will outlast me?
3. What changes will I make today that will begin to demonstrate a life "in perspective"?

Notes

1. Reflection from Oscar Romero, www.aggiecatholic.org/resources/prayers/reflection

Chapter 16

Know what you are meant to be doing

Let me refer again to a training day for headteachers I recently attended in the London area. I wasn't thinking of becoming a headteacher (in fact, the more the day went on, the more my respect for them grew and the more grateful I was that I wasn't one!) but I *was* interested in some of the principles that helped them survive in a very demanding profession. At one point, the speaker at the conference shared with us that a recent poll had uncovered the fact that 80 per cent of American managers cannot answer with any measure of confidence these three simple questions:

- What is my job?
- What in my job really counts?
- How well am I doing?

I must have missed the next part of the teaching as I began to apply what I had heard to my own experience. I realized that for a good part of my ministry and church leadership, I could not have answered those questions either. And I suspected that most of the leaders I know almost certainly could not do so either. If that is even partially true, how can a person, whether a headteacher or a leader in a church, hope to survive without knowing these things? Surely, it would be a recipe for massive discouragement and eventually lead to a desire to get out.

You might reply to the first question, "I know my job. I am the pastor of the church." But that is not your job. That is your position or title. The question is really, "What are you personally meant to be doing and achieving?"

As with a headteacher, you might come back defensively with a huge list of things that it might mean and probably does at some point or other. You may have a "job description" but that may not fully answer the question. Herein lies the problem of church leadership. It can easily become a job without definition and without boundaries and therefore you can never work out if you are doing OK or not, or when the job is done. That is only one step away from disillusionment and depression. I remember telling someone that I "ran a church" but as I said it I thought, "Is that really what I do? It isn't what I intended and anyway what does it mean?"

In his excellent book entitled *Leading in a Culture of Change*[1], Michael Fullan suggests that a primary driver in leadership is what he calls "moral purpose". This refers to the motivation of bringing about betterment in others. Without it, leaders will not survive. I would suggest that if we are looking for a way of defining our job it must have something to do with bringing about change in others. For a teacher to see a "no hope" pupil attain what for that child are great achievements must be a most powerful stimulus to get up in the morning and keep going.

Could it be that the job for everyone in church leadership is actually the same? Could it be that "making disciples" is in fact the thing that we are all about? The gifts we have to enable us to accomplish that goal may be different but that is the "moral purpose". If we take making disciples as the central task, we can actually find out how we are doing.

The second question, "What in my job really counts?", is the heart of the matter. If we really knew the answer to that, then that is what we would concentrate on – or would we, in a life of multiple demands? If we don't get to the heart of the matter we will never achieve what we are here to do. Once you know what your job is, what you're actually there to be and do, and follow this up with a disciplined, boundary-setting lifestyle, then you should achieve not only success but fulfilment. To do what counts may mean that some things don't get done, but nobody will mind if lives are being changed.

The third question is one that many leaders never stop to ask. They work on the basis that if nobody is complaining then they are probably doing OK. The question is whether OK is OK. What if you are only average at your job but you have the potential to be outstanding? You will never have the thrill of being outstanding if being average gets you by. In church life, we always want to see people develop and grow in their gifts and abilities but what about the leader? How do you monitor your own progress? Do you even want to know? Does it really matter if you don't do the job as well as you could do it? Actually, yes, it does. It matters to everyone else and, in fact, it matters to you. You will always experience greater pleasure in life when you are using and developing your gifts and talents to the best possible extent.

So, it may prove worthwhile to find out from time to time how you are doing. The simplest way is to ask for the opinion of people that you can trust and who will share with you from a loving perspective. But this is not always possible. You may have to devise your own system of self-appraisal if one is not already in place.

The most important thing is to be looking to improve and never settling for how well you do the job now. John Kotter, a business consultant from Harvard, has come up with a great way of understanding how to be more effective. He says that the natural inclination if you do not feel you are being effective is to apply more effort. So we work harder, longer hours and push other people to do the same.

The chart below shows the relationship between ability and effort. With much effort and low ability, effectiveness is low. If you try and increase the effort, the increase in effect is rather small. But, if instead of just trying harder you increase ability, effectiveness is hugely increased with very little extra effort.

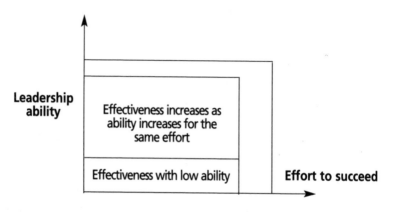

The lesson for all of us in any area of leadership is that it is always better to sharpen our skills than apply more work hours. We all have things we can learn. There are people who have been in the game longer, those who have stumbled on good practice that we do not know about. There are often very simple things that can be done and that make a huge difference without doing very much extra. But in all of this we require humility to acknowledge we could do better, and a willingness to always be learners. I think I have learnt more about leadership in the last few years than in all the previous years put together. The reason for this was that I did not know where to look for help and was so caught up with *what* I was doing, I did not stop to ask the question about *how* I was doing.

You are unlikely to survive leadership if you don't know what you are meant to be doing or take time to evaluate how you are doing.

Stop for a moment and consider:

1. **What is my job as a leader? Write it down.**
2. **What in this job really counts?**
3. **How well am I doing?**
4. **Who will I ask about this?**
5. **What changes will I now make?**

Notes

1. Michael Fullan, *Leading in a Culture of Change*, San Francisco, Jossey-Bass, 2001.

Chapter 17

Encourage younger leaders

This principle is particularly relevant to those who have been in leadership for some time, but good for us all to bear in mind.

As I mentioned in the introduction, I moved to Birmingham at the age of 24 years at the request of David MacInnes, an Anglican minister who was a member of the Cathedral staff but had a call and ministry across the city. We already knew one another as I had come to faith through hearing him speak while still at school. He asked Lois and me to come to the city to develop the work amongst young people (purely because of a gut feeling he had that there was going to be a significant work in that area). He thought that some leadership involving someone nearer them in age would be required. I had no previous experience of youth work but I was young and full of enthusiasm about my faith.

I learned a great deal about low-key mentoring from David and how to take risks with younger people. Now that it is my turn to do the same I realize it is not that easy. David gave a free hand to me and another young man to get on with whatever we thought best to do, as long as it was under the overall brief of helping young people find faith and grow as Christians, but he was always there for advice and help. As it turned out, we had arrived on the edge of an extraordinary revival among young people in the city which is a story in itself. It proved to be an amazing time when almost anything we tried, worked. We did out-of-the-ordinary things and took huge risks, even buying a large property in the centre of the city when we had almost no money.

I do not remember any occasions when David sat me down and said, "Today we are going to have a leadership training session. Get out your notebook and pen and listen carefully. At the end of this session, I want you to write a 10,000-word paper on 'evangelising young people in an urban environment'." Now, there is nothing wrong with classroom learning, and the discipline of writing essays to focus the mind is a very valuable exercise. However, to be pushed into the deep end and to discover for yourself the same valuable lessons has a far deeper impact. Due to the size of what was happening, the things we got involved in reflected back on David because he was well known in the city. Anything that went well was attributed to him and by implication to those who worked with him, but conversely, whenever things went wrong, he took the blame. In other words, he was willing to put his reputation on the line for the sake of a group of rather enthusiastic but inexperienced young people. But this was the means by which leadership skills, in this case, were allowed to develop. It also meant that when he was no longer able to give time to this ministry because of a call to other things, the work went on, as he was not indispensable.

When David eventually moved to another work elsewhere, it left an emotional hole in my heart. Although we had not worked closely for some time, I had developed a close bond with him and always felt his supportive presence. Nevertheless, his leaving caused growth in me as I discovered that I could do the work without him. He had been a real spiritual father to me and I owe him more than I can say.

Now, many years later, I realize how hard a thing it is to release others and be there for them. It becomes difficult to let others do what you have become skilled in. You think it won't be done so well. You are tempted to keep control of it all, so that no mistakes are made, but you end up being the only person who can do things. Having said that, there is only one thing more difficult than handing over and finding a thing done worse and that is handing over and discovering it is done better! If we are honest, most leaders find that both encouraging and threatening.

It is often said that at the age of thirteen, many boys become more accomplished at sport than their fathers. Some fathers cannot cope with this and try to dominate their children rather than let their own egos be damaged. A wise father, however, recognizes growth in his son and lets him go past him with pride and joy. There are few more rewarding things in life (if your pride can take it) than seeing a younger person receive more praise than yourself in your own area of gifting, knowing they achieved success because you gave them room. It means you have assured the continuation of the ministry entrusted to you.

You may know leaders who are so keen to continue their ministry to the bitter end, that when their time comes to leave or retire, there is no one there to take over. That is why we have this extraordinary system of "hiring in" from outside. It is nearly always disruptive to a church or any organization but it is the pattern in most of the Western church and one we have exported around the world. Jim Collins, an American researcher who examined businesses that achieved "greatness" by his criteria, discovered that amongst his "good to great" companies not one hired their chief executive from outside. In fact, others that did this always faced major disruptive consequences. However, this pattern has become the norm for church life and it is one of the reasons for the weariness and tiredness of leaders. Many just cannot let go. We need to be nurturing younger leaders, some of whom may leave us to develop new works elsewhere whilst others stay to take the reins at home.

Most younger leaders grow for two reasons. Firstly, they see someone that they resonate with (often of similar gifting), and then they watch them, follow them and even mimic them for a time until they find their own natural style. Secondly, they are given responsibility with some accountability. The key is that responsibility comes with empowerment to do the job and the freedom to get it wrong.

Jesus was, of course, the greatest example of this. He entrusted the future of his mission to a bunch of young men who were in the main uneducated and on the surface ill-equipped for the job. But they lived with him, watched him, listened to him and then he sent them off to have a go themselves. He was prepared to take the flak for their mistakes and put his reputation on the line. He debriefed them and encouraged them in what they had done. Then, when the time came for him to leave, after only three years, they were ready to take over. It is amazing that he believed that this group could get the job done (empowered, of course, by the Holy Spirit).

Unfortunately, we in the present day are not good at finding ways to provide academic training *in situ* so the college format seems the only way for most who want to go into full-time ministry.

In the Western church, particularly in Europe, there is increasingly a missing generation, those aged between 18 and 30. Not only is this the group who have "never been to church" and are outside the catchment of the church, but fewer and fewer congregations have many members from this age group. Culture is changing so fast that to understand this age group, and younger people, and to be able to communicate with them, will, in the main but not exclusively, need people a little older to take the lead. Unless this happens, the situation will become very serious. If ever there was a time to release younger people into leadership it is now. It doesn't even have to be overall leadership. It could be part of a team.

It is easy to write like this but I am aware how hard it has been to choose to do so. Even if you have plenty of examples to follow, when it comes to your turn, you find that leadership becomes sticky in your hand. How hard it is to take the risks of releasing others, taking the consequences of mistakes and being there to encourage and let go again! It always seems easiest to do it yourself, especially as you become more accomplished and relaxed in what you do.

Without releasing others, though, your leadership will not survive. You will eventually become tired and weary but less and less able to let go because you have become indispensable. When you eventually have to go, there may be no one waiting in the wings. But it does not have to be this way.

If you are willing to let younger people express their youthful, visionary hearts but keep a loose hold so that you can prevent disaster, you will not only have relieved yourself of work, but released huge potential into the future.

It is unlikely that you will survive leadership if you are not prepared to release younger people into ministry and leadership.

Stop for a moment and consider:

1. **What younger person have I encouraged to take responsibility?**
2. **Who is looking to me for fatherly/motherly help?**
3. **What will I do today to set this in motion?**
4. **What risks am I prepared to take and with whom?**

Chapter 18
Never walk alone

Many of the pressures we have been discussing come from lone ministry. It would appear from Scripture that it was never intended to be that way. From the very beginning, Jesus sent the disciples out in twos, and he never expected them to go alone. In fact, he himself did not go alone but chose a team to be with him all through his ministry. When Paul went on his missionary journeys, he travelled with others. When he appointed leaders over the church, he appointed elders, not just a lone leader.

The gift of leadership may be given to an individual but it was never intended to function in isolation. It is a strange thing that if you work with a buddy, it more than halves the load. It is like leaning back against someone. You both take the weight so it almost feels like neither of you is taking it. You both offload the weight of responsibility onto each other and it makes the whole load feel lighter. To have companionship makes such a difference.

Even though there may be a recognized leader and defined gifting and ministries, all leadership in church should be expressed in a team. There are so many advantages for everyone concerned. The main problem, however, is that although we may agree with the idea, most teams are not teams at all; they are committees. The committee causes strain in one of two ways. Either it is made up of people who each represent an area of church life and are fighting their own corner (none carry the overall vision and therefore the leader continues to shoulder the burden alone), or it is made up of people whose main work is elsewhere outside the church but who have been invited on to the parish church council, elders' board or whatever. They are full of advice, but at the end of the day, you go home feeling you have been dumped upon by well-meaning people who do not live with the issues important to you, and you have more to do than when you started!

The essence of teamwork is quite different. The following expresses the heart of what a team really is.

It is made up of a group of people who all have their own areas of responsibility but who also feel responsible for the whole. It is a group in which everyone, including the leader, is mutually accountable; in which there is freedom to disagree strongly but without breaking relationship; and in which the aims and goals are able to be evaluated clearly. It is genuinely a team if everyone is pulling in the same direction and all members feel responsible.

It is the difference between watching a bunch of school-children apparently playing football, but all chasing the ball in one huge group, all wanting to score the goal and with very little sense of working together, and a professional football team with common purpose, each fulfilling their part with an agreed objective.

A leader working in the latter type of environment is at peace, not only because they are sharing a load, but also because they are probably enjoying themselves. I have been in both situations, although never fully experiencing the latter as I should. When I did, it was a great place to be.

That is how church leadership should feel. It is not a denial of leadership gifting; it is the right understanding of the context in which it best operates. It is also so much better if a team can stay together as long as possible. If the following excerpt from the works of Gaius Petronius is anything to go by (written 2,000 years ago), there has obviously been a problem in this area for a long time...

> We trained hard but it seemed every time we were beginning to form up into teams we were reorganized. I was to learn later in life that we tend to meet any situation by reorganizing, and what a wonderful method it can be for creating the illusion of progress while producing confusion, inefficiency and demoralization.[1]

Not only is working as a team the best way for church leadership, but it is also the best for itinerant ministry as well. As I have travelled around in ministry, I have often done so alone but there have been many occasions where I have taken a team from the church and it has been a real team. I am in no doubt which of the two is preferable. The team is so much more fun and so much more relaxing. Although I have appeared to onlookers to be the key person as the speaker, I have known that I would not have been anywhere near as effective without the team.

It has been interesting to give a closer examination to certain situations where I had assumed the effectiveness of a particular work was due to the outstanding gifts of a particular individual whose name was always associated with that work. In such situations I have often found that alongside that person was a deeply committed team all pulling together for the same purpose and goals but happy for the leader to receive public recognition. It is these same ministries that have the capacity to continue when the leader has to move on for some reason or other. It also means that when the leader is away, life goes on.

If a team such as this is just not possible, then at least a partnership should be sought after. Find someone with whom you can share the load, with whom you can laugh and cry. Find someone with different gifts and strengths from your own, so that you won't feel in competition but will enjoy what each partner brings. How do you find such a person or people? I know it's difficult, but if you start from the principle that this is what God intended and you strongly desire it, I think it is highly likely that God will bring it together.

You will find it difficult to survive for long in leadership if you don't work in the context of a team.

Stop for a moment and consider:

1. **Do I work with teams or committees?**
2. **Am I alone in my leadership or do I have heart companions?**
3. **If I am alone, what am I going to do to bring about a change?**

Notes

1. Michael Fullan, *Leading in a Culture of Change*, San Francisco, Jossey-Bass, 2001.

Chapter 19

Face your losses and move on

W e leant heavily on the back door of the van and eventually, after a lot of pushing and shoving, it clicked closed. Our son and daughter-in-law said goodbye and drove away to unpack all the van's contents again at their new flat in London. I went up to the top of the house to my son's bedroom to check that everything had indeed been packed. I sat on the mattress on the bed in the empty room and burst into tears. I just cried and cried. After some time alone, Lois joined me in the room. "He's gone. He has finally gone!" I sobbed and she joined me in shared tears. It didn't last long but I felt washed clean by the tears.

Andrew had left home many times and come back, but this was final as he had always left most of his belongings here in "his" room. Now they were gone. He was married, and he was gone. He would be back to visit but it would be on a different basis.

I was so glad of that unexpected time in my son's room. I had not until then really come to terms with the loss. When each of our boys went to university for their first term, we had shed our tears because we knew it would never be the same again and we had to own that loss too.

Life is a series of losses. When you marry, you lose independence. When you start work, you lose freedom. When you get sick, you lose health. When loved ones die, you lose companionship. When you lose your job, you lose a sense of security. As you get older, you lose physical strength and stamina and often your health. You lose your youth. Life is full of losses and new gains, but at the time of change the loss always seems harder than the joy of the new.

Church life and leadership is exactly the same. It is full of losses as things move on. People leave – a loss. You move – a loss. Expectations are not fulfilled, you are let down, your role changes, you let go to younger people so you can move on. Every stage brings with it a realization that something we once had treasured and relied on is gone. It leaves a real hole in your emotional make-up. It leaves a sense of emptiness.

In this situation there are two equal and opposite errors to make. One is to deny the reality of the loss, to put on a brave face, to shrug your shoulders and quickly move on, suppressing any pain you may feel. This is not at all uncommon in Christian circles, particularly amongst leaders who have a "living in victory" mentality that believes owning up to pain and confusion is somehow a state of spiritual failure. The other error is to live in the pain and never come out of it. This happens very much in bereavement. There is a well-recognized pattern that follows loss: shock, disbelief, denial, anger, bitterness but, finally, hopefully, acceptance and moving on.

It is the accumulation of unresolved losses over many years that leads to depression in a large number of people, especially Christian leaders. In the USA, it has been estimated that as many as one in eight church leaders is clinically depressed, and one in four youth leaders. There will of course be many reasons for this but high on the list will be the inability to deal with loss and disappointment. Every loss needs to be owned. Every loss needs to be grieved appropriately and honestly and every loss needs to be left behind. If it is not left behind, you will carry it like a dead weight through your life and it will accumulate other unresolved pain along the way until it eventually stops you functioning altogether.

We need to begin by acknowledging that to be a Christian is to be fully human. That means to face the reality that we are feeling, thinking, choosing, spiritual beings. In the emotional life we feel real pain. Life hurts and that is how it is. To be a spiritual person does not mean that we have to live permanently happy and confessing that all is always well. In the words of the beautiful song by the band REM, "everybody hurts sometimes," and that is because we are human and God made us sensitive. To deny that sensitivity is to deny our God-given make-up and to inflict incredible damage on ourselves. Men from my background suffer a double problem both from the ethos taught to us when we were young, "real men don't cry," and from the Christian church that often demands unreality.

The second error is equally common in Christian circles. It is caused by continuing to live in pain and wallowing in self-pity. This is to deny the power of the cross to take our pain and the presence of the Spirit to carry us on to a new day. Real healing and therefore health in life comes from being able to face, own and acknowledge the loss and the pain. Then we must grieve it and, as much as we are able to, express it with emotion and tears. Then we must move on, leaving the loss behind, never to be revisited except as a fact of our history.

To do this well, we need community to help us. It is hard to do it alone. That is what church is all about. It is having people around us who can share the pain of our losses but help us to mark a line in the sand and move on.

As I write this I am reminded of an article in the national press that I read recently about a man whose son was born with Down's syndrome. This man had longed for a son with whom he could do all the things fathers love to do with their sons – play football, teach them to fish – but he realized his dreams were shattered. He became so angry he even left his wife for a time. The story has a happy ending as he shared how he had to face his loss head-on, weep over it and move on. That actually led to a deep love and affection between himself and the boy, which previously would always have been tainted by resentment.

I believe the Christian ministry has the potential to be a place of huge pain. It is so filled with expectations, longings and dreams that it is wide open to disappointment and discouragement. We are always dependent on the behaviour of other people, many of whom will let us down because our expectations are too high. Many will behave in a way that will cause us loss. If we can learn to deal with the losses along the way, that may go a long way to providing a means of making it through.

The very exciting thing about all of this is that the other side of every loss is a very real gain. The sad thing is to never enjoy the gain because you cannot let go of the past. How can we enjoy our freedom and release to new things at the same time as seeing younger people prosper if we will not let go of leadership? If we don't let go but live forever in the pain of loss, our new life will never be enjoyed to the full.

In conclusion, here are some steps forward:

- Discover and acknowledge your loss;
- Say goodbye to it (with tears if necessary);
- Let it go;
- Move on and don't look back.

You will never survive leadership if you do not learn to deal with the losses in your life.

Stop for a moment and consider:

1. What losses have I had in my life?
2. What losses am I facing now?
3. Have I processed each of these and am I moving on?
4. Who is helping me to do this?
5. What will I do today that will help me move into tomorrow without the burden of loss?

Chapter 20

Understand stress

Why do so many in ministry feel not only tired but also depressed on Mondays? Why do we feel tired after a week's holiday? How can I feel so good one moment and so low another? We all have different temperaments and react differently but it is all too easy in Christian ministry to interpret everything with a so-called "spiritual" solution. Very often our problems are not spiritual at all, merely physical. We are experiencing our body responding in its normal, God-ordained way. The great need is to understand what is going on and to learn to manage it, rather than fighting it. I wish I had known this years ago.

I personally have been greatly helped by the insights of Dr Archibald Hart who is a practising clinical psychologist and also on the staff of Fuller Theological Seminary in California. He has done extensive research on the causes of stress and written a number of helpful books on the subject. He writes,

We live within a body that responds to stress and in a world that produces it. The potential for stress is all about us – in our friends, families, work, in every part of our life. Our bodies are intricately designed to respond to stress in such a way as to help us cope with it, at least initially. Each of us is equipped with a highly sophisticated defence system designed to help against threats that would destroy us and to help us cope with those events that would challenge us. The stress response system is comprised of a complex array of hormones and instinctive responses that ensure our survival.

Whenever we are threatened physically or psychologically,

> a chain of responses is set in motion to prepare us for what has been described as the "fight or flight" response. Behind it all is this wonderful adrenal system with its complex assortment of hormones.[1]

In other words the effects of stress on each of us individually are caused by the release of adrenaline into our system as a result of our body preparing for action. So, for example, when we prepare to preach on a Sunday, adrenaline causes our blood pressure to rise and pulse rate to increase to prepare us for action. There is nothing wrong with short bursts of adrenaline response – indeed we were made for it – but it is the long-term relentless state of pressure with its resultant continual hormonal high that has serious effects on the cardiovascular system. However, adrenaline rush, even in the short term, will cause an equal and opposite reaction in the body, known as "post-adrenaline depression". Its symptoms can be irritability, negativity and a general sense of weariness and fatigue. This reaction is a "friend" to the body. It is saying, in effect, "the crisis is over, we are no longer on readiness alert for any eventuality, so let's relax." What is then needed is recovery time. The main cause of stress-related illness today is the failure to give the body recovery time.

One of the dangers of an adrenaline-induced high, is that you may well feel good, in fact, very good. As we all like to feel good, we will do what we can to either achieve that state of high and/or stay there as long as possible. So we find ourselves saying, "This cannot possibly be doing me harm. I feel so good."

The secret here is to both understand our bodies and also to appreciate that we have this "treasure in a jar of clay". We need to look after ourselves and function within our God-given limitations or we will have to experience the consequences.

Now back to Monday morning! If you have preached on Sunday morning, come the afternoon you may feel very tired. If you are then out again at night, by the end of the day you will have had a lot of adrenaline flowing through the system. By Monday you will be in a post-adrenaline state and may feel rather irritable and negative about things, particularly about your sermon the day before! This is a reason why many people have suggested that Monday is a poor day to have as a day off. It is a good day to do fairly light work. Then fully enjoy a day off when you are recovered later in the week.

The key in all of this is to understand what your body is doing and what it is telling you. If you understand why you feel the way you do, you can begin to manage yourself so that you enable your life to have a sense of rhythm. If we are going to live a life with many potential stress factors, including public speaking and dealing with people's emotional issues, we need to learn how to relax and let our bodies recover.

Hart suggests five steps to manage stress:

- Find a sensitive method for monitoring stress levels, e.g. take pulse rate, check hands to face to see if cold (often a sign of stress).
- Think conservation. Put adrenaline-lowering strategies in place in your life, e.g. always build in rest times after very active times.
- Learn relaxation techniques.
- Set boundaries on your life so you are able to say "no".
- Improve the quality of your sleep, preferably – for most people – eight to nine hours.

I've found as I've got older and more aware of my limitations, that I have had to set quite clear boundaries on such things as the number of speaking engagements in a week or weekend, length of travel without staying away overnight, or number of events in one day. I now know that if I overdo it, I will pay for it later. I used to be very bad at stacking up meetings. At the time I arranged them, I thought it would be no problem, but later I would wonder why I felt not just weary but also depressed. Lois used to get tired of my saying, "I don't know why I feel so tired. I know I've been doing a lot but I've been enjoying it!" The "enjoying it" part was giving me a great adrenaline high.

It is noticeable that in the period of Jesus' ministry, he regularly set aside times to "go apart and rest" with his closest friends. Although in some ways his life was free of many of the present pressures in terms of speed of change and choice, he had his own set of unusual pressures but still determined to keep to his boundaries ("I only do what I see the Father doing", "I am sent to...", "My time has not yet come", etc.). It is obvious too, that Jesus was not willing to give in to the urgent over the important, and that he enjoyed the journey as well as the destination. These are two sure ways to lessen the stress of life.

There are so many in ministry who do not learn either to understand themselves or put boundaries in their life when they are young. For years they appear to get away with it and then, in midlife, they begin to realize the consequences of not respecting their body's needs. The internal damage never appears until it is almost too late. When we are young, we feel there is no limit to what we can do and that may be true but we cannot abuse the body without consequences. It will catch up with us at some point. The tortoise often outruns the hare in the end. The person who is careful with his or her body may appear to achieve less but is often still going strong long after the others have had to drop out of the race.

Understanding the effects and workings of adrenaline in my body has helped me appreciate why I feel the way I do and has begun to teach me to build in pauses as well as activity.

It is also well worth noting the important fact that there is much evidence to suggest that we are at our most inventive and creative when we are at a low level of adrenaline arousal. Many people find they have their most creative times in the bath or shower, or that a thought comes to them when they are lying in bed at night. That is why you would do well to have a pad and pen by the bed so you can write things down before you forget. There is a law (known as the Yerkes-Dodson law), which states that:

- At low adrenaline arousal we are not very effective in action but very good at thinking creatively;
- At medium arousal, we become more effective in action and less in creative thinking;
- At high arousal, our efficiency in both action and thinking drops off again.

So here is another reason to lower stress levels at least for a time. As you do so, more creativity will flow. The time you take "off" for leisure and relaxation may turn out to be the most creative time you have. You might even initially be frustrated that while you are trying to rest, thoughts come to your mind, but you should rejoice in them. If you then write them down you are spared the necessity of dashing off to fulfil your new ideas. That can wait until you are ready for action again.

You will find it hard to survive leadership and finish the course if you do not understand your body and learn to go with its flow.

Stop for a moment and consider:

1. Looking at the pattern of my life, am I building in recovery time?
2. What really energizes me and gives me a buzz?
3. What am I doing to make sure I do not stay "high" for too long?
4. When have I felt most low, does that coincide with an adrenaline drop?
5. How will I change to manage my rhythm better?

Notes

1. Dr Archibald D. Hart, *Adrenalin and Stress*, Nashville, W Publishing Group, 1995.

Chapter 21

Stay at peace in a sea of change

Eddie Gibbs, a lecturer at Fuller Theological Seminary, made the following comment on the effect of living in what is becoming a post-Christendom society, particularly in Western Europe:

> The result is a generation of leaders who do not know how to lead within a context of rapid and chaotic change. We were trained to map-read on well-marked roads, not navigate on stormy seas. I believe the changes are significant and irreversible – while tomorrow continues to arrive ahead of schedule, yesterday can never be revisited.

Brian McLaren, in *The Church on the Other Side*, writes,

> You and I happen to be born at an "edge," at a time of high "tectonic" activity in history – the end of one age and the beginning of another. It is a time of shaking. Yesterday's maps are outdated, and today's will soon be too.[1]

This is a very disorienting time to be in church ministry. The trouble is that we think we should know what to do. The truth is that we, along with everyone else, have not been this way before and we don't know what to do. This can and will make leading incredibly wearing and difficult, because not only do people want us to tell them where we are going, but we too would like to be more sure of where it is all heading.

In years gone by, Christian leadership was comparatively straightforward because life was pretty consistent. It isn't any more. We are on a rollercoaster ride. There are books beginning to tumble into the bookshops concerning the problems of being post-everything. In other words, what we have known for so long is now disappearing and just as you thought you knew what you were doing and how things work, it is all shifting sand. There are plenty of people beginning to tell us what shape or shapes the church might be in the future and that can bring an unnecessary pressure. Can I make a few suggestions?

Be willing to admit you do not know the answers

It is helpful to know what the questions are but do not rush into quick conclusions. I spoke a short time ago at a celebration meeting in the south of England and was describing many of the changes taking place in the world as it affects the future of the church. I then commented that although I had a few ideas, I really I had no idea where we were actually heading, what the end product would look like or what to do to get there. I was inundated with leaders who said they felt the same way but hadn't the courage to say so. They assumed that to be a leader meant that you knew everything and that to admit confusion was to fail.

One popular writer on leadership in the business world has said, "A great leader does not have to come up with all the answers and then motivate everyone to follow his messianic vision. But it does mean having the humility to grasp the fact that you do not yet understand enough to have the answers and then be willing to ask the questions that will lead to the best possible insights."[2]

Can you imagine how clueless the first disciples were

when the church was first formed? Having just got a handle on things in the early days, the church was then dispersed and it was all change. Then the Gentile world started to get reached and things were different again. (That leads to my second suggestion below.) Be encouraged that although you may be bewildered by the changes, God isn't. He is capable of reaching any culture at any time.

Be willing to take on new ideas

This really means being willing to drop cherished ways of doing things. There are obviously principles learned over years and grounded in the Bible that will never change. But culture (the way we do things around here) is changing. What worked well in one situation may well not work in another. Paul said, "forgetting what lies behind..." That is not to dismiss the past, but the blessings of another time can lock us into patterns and ways that prevent us being effective in the present. It requires humility to acknowledge there may be things we don't understand.

In the late 1970s and 80s, I was very involved in university ministry. After a time, I thought I knew the best way to approach students. Now things have changed. What we did then, in the main, will not work today. The blessing of the past was great but that is exactly what it was: the past. I cannot afford to stay there polishing my medals and looking at the photos. It is great to give thanks but we must move on.

Loosen your grip on the church

I do not mean by this that we are to let go of leadership, but that many of us would do well to have a lighter touch. When Jesus said, "I will build my church and the gates of hell will not prevail against it," we may not know exactly what he meant but one thing is pretty clear and that is that he himself was going to be responsible for building the church. The weight that sits so heavily on most leaders is the problem of responsibility for the church. We even talk about it as "my church" or "so-and-so's church". It is actually Jesus' church and he is building it in the way that he sees fit. When everything was going apparently remarkably well in the first period after Pentecost, he decided to break it apart. One day it was a church of thousands – a mega-church, no less – and the next it was almost nothing. Jesus knew best how the culture would be reached.

We are in for a very untidy time and for those of us who like order, it could be very uncomfortable unless we loosen our grip. This will only happen if leaders let people have freedom to take risks and develop new things, free of heavy control. And if you have that attitude of letting go, and trusting Jesus with his church, you are far more likely to survive this very unsettled time.

There are two principles that I have learned from playing golf that apply to our lives. The problem with golf is that it is a "mind over matter" game. Even though you think you have grasped something with your mind, when it actually comes to it, your body reverts to its natural way of behaving. If you watched me play, I think you would have to admit that my practice swing is pretty good. In fact, I think I could turn professional on my practice swing! But the real thing, played only moments later in the same position by the same person, is a completely different matter – the only difference being that when there is a ball in front of me, it is for real.

I am beginning to learn two things and they are pertinent here even if you have no interest in the game of golf.

1. **Soft hands! That means, hold the club loosely.** Most players, like me, tighten their grip when they try to hit the ball. In ministry, we all like the idea of sitting loose to the church but when it comes to it, we hold it tight. We can tell how tight we hold it by the pressure and tension it causes us, especially when things go wrong. You do not own the church, it is not yours and you are not finally responsible, so loosen your grip and let it hang loose a little.

2. **Let the club-head do the work!** Golf clubs are designed so that they hit the ball the correct distance without huge effort. You may well believe that in theory, but in actual fact you believe it has to do with human effort and strength. It never works well that way. Sometimes, the harder you try, the worse it gets! In ministry, as in all Christian living, the key is to "let the Godhead do the work". That does not take away human responsibility but does take away the strain. God is running the universe. He is in charge. He has everything under control. He loves you personally, intimately, unconditionally and continually. Let him work and stop worrying.

   Jesus loves the church. It is his Bride. Let him deal with it. The Holy Spirit is at work. He changes lives, convicts of sin, heals and guides. Let him do what he was sent to do. All we are expected to do is cooperate with the Godhead, not take his place just in case. Let God do what he wants to do and relax into him. Sounds easy, doesn't it? Golf looks incredibly easy when you watch the professionals. They have worked hard at relaxing into the game. We need to strive to enter the rest of God.

The other side of all this is to concentrate on the thing Jesus did command us to do and that is to "make disciples". That is our job specification.

Immerse yourself in two worlds but only have your heart in one

In recent years, the life of Daniel has been quite significant to me as a model of Christian leadership and discipleship in the 21st century. Living in Babylon, he was out of his natural and familiar territory. He chose to be fully involved with the culture in which he found himself. He studied it, understood it and did his best to be a part of it. Importantly, though, he went three times a day to his room, where an open window faced Jerusalem. Daniel lived in the culture of Babylon but his heart was towards Jerusalem. He filled his mind and heart with the realities of the living God and that helped him live "supernaturally naturally" in an alien culture.

If we are to be effective leaders, we should not be afraid of being in the culture of our time but we will need to keep our hearts immersed in God. That's the place of peace and tranquillity. We can cope with all the uncertainties of the world around us if, at the end of the day, we spend time practising the presence of God and meditating on the things of his Kingdom whose fullness is yet to be revealed.

Stop for a moment and consider:

1. What most confuses me about the present changes in culture?
2. How am I seeking to understand what is going on?
3. What are the key questions to be asking?
4. What would "hold the church loosely" mean for me?

Notes

1. Brian McLaren, *The Church on the Other Side,* Grand Rapids, Zondervan, 2003.
2. Jim Collins, *Good to Great,* London, Random House Business Books, 2001.

Chapter 22

Avoid burnout

Stress and burnout are not the same thing. Stress is defined in terms of the response of your body to demands made on it. Burnout is a form of emotional exhaustion or, as Archibald Hart calls it, "compassion fatigue". The term was first coined by a New York psychologist, Herbert J. Freudenberger, in the 1970s, to describe the symptoms of severe drug addicts. He then began to study similar symptoms in people of the caring professions and he used the term "burnout" to describe what he saw as "a state of depleted physical and mental resources" i.e. a person feels as if they have come to the end of the line. They can go no further.

"A burned-out person becomes tired and frustrated often by striving to reach an unrealistic goal or by devotion to a cause, a way of life, or a relationship that has failed to produce the expected reward." This describes much of the ministry carried out in the late 20th and early 21st centuries, particularly in the Western world.

Christina Maslach, professor of psychology at the University of California Berkeley, is an expert in this field and has described burnout in these terms, "Burnout is the index of the dislocation between what people are and what they have to do. It represents an erosion in values, dignity, spirit, and will – an erosion of the human soul. It is a malady that spreads gradually and continuously over time, putting people into a downward spiral from which it is hard to recover." You can easily see from this that it is very likely to affect people in Christian ministry, particularly those who are achievers, or go-getters, and those who care for the needs of others. It is also important to note that it is not a problem like catching a cold, where a few days off will do the trick. Because of the seriousness and the long-term effects of the problem it is vital that a pattern of life is adopted that will prevent this ever happening.

In their book, *Beyond Burnout: How to Enjoy Your Job Again When You've Just About Had Enough[1]*, authors David Welch, Donald Medeiros and George Tate compare a healthy person to a burned-out person in five major areas.

- Physically, a healthy person has energy, whereas a burned-out person is unmotivated and experiences exhaustion and stress disease.
- Intellectually, a healthy person is creative and sharp, whereas a burned-out person is cynical.
- Emotionally, a healthy person is optimistic, patient and has empathy and sensitivity to others, whereas a burned-out person is depressed, aloof, distant and mentally and emotionally exhausted.
- Socially, a healthy person is engaged and involved in the lives of others, whereas a burned-out person is withdrawn, or exhibits inappropriate behaviour or hostility.
- Spiritually, a healthy person has joy and a sense of purpose, but a burned-out person lacks meaning and purpose.

Someone else has written, "A sense of uncontrollability or helplessness is the final stage of burnout and is accompanied by depression and feelings of futility."[2]

It needs to be said at this point that any of these symptoms can be experienced without being caused by burnout. It is always advisable to go to seek professional medical advice when you are not feeling as you should. Very often, there is a simple physical reason for the problem, which can be remedied.

It is also important to say that it is very foolish to wait until you get to experience the symptoms of burnout before you do anything about your lifestyle. The crash may come in your forties and fifties but the groundwork will almost certainly be laid in the earlier years. If you are young, begin to build patterns of behaviour that will enable you to go for the long haul.

I remember well hearing a young, enthusiastic preacher say from the pulpit, "I would rather burn out for Jesus than rust out!" It sounded terrific but when you stop to think about it, whether you burn out or rust out, it is still "out". After all, finishing the race is what is important and to do so may mean to run it more slowly and appear to achieve less along the way. There are far too many who have begun well and never made it to the end. Their life's work will be cut short by ill health.

Most of what is written in this book is designed to prevent burnout. But here are the main keys:

1. **Maintain spiritual disciplines.** Set aside daily times of quiet for prayer, meditation, reading and space to "be". We neglect this at our peril. It is very common for those in "full-time" ministry to fail to give quality time to themselves other than for sermon preparation or preparing for some meeting or other. Do an honesty check on yourself.

2. **Expect life to be hard.** M. Scott Peck points out in his book, *The Road Less Travelled*[3], that when you expect life to be difficult, it is much less difficult. That, by the way, is very different from being a pessimist; it is being a realist about life. A friend who works in a poor part of Africa told me, "The difference between Westerners and the people

here is that in the West you expect your car to go and never break down, and when it does you are angry and frustrated. Here, no one expects their car to work properly, so when it doesn't, they are not surprised, but when it does, they are delighted! That's why they experience more joy than you do."

3. **Take regular time off.** One day off a week should be minimum for every person in full-time leadership. Wednesday or Thursday is best for preachers – away from the adrenaline rush of Sunday. Most people in ordinary work situations will get the weekend off, but if that is full of ministry, there should be another day. This is not a "nice idea if you can do it". It is essential for survival. You cannot afford to go without it. On your days off, do something very different from what you would do on other days.

Take the full annual leave. If at all possible, get at least three weeks at one time, once a year. If you are married, have overnighters away with your spouse on a regular basis.

In a lecture entitled "The Minister's Fainting Fits" C.H. Spurgeon said, "Repose is as needful to the mind as sleep to the body... if we do not rest, we shall break down."

4. **Get proper exercise and sleep.** Exercise at least three to four times a week for at least half an hour. Walk, swim, play sport, get the heart going faster for a period of time. Most people need at least eight hours of sleep a night.

5. **Be part of a peer group for prayer, sharing and friendship.** A place to laugh and cry is essential for all in leadership. You will not survive without it. You need to

have a place to unburden yourself, and to receive prayer, where you are not the leader or the minister. If you do not have such a group, work at one as soon as possible. Nobody is expected to make it on their own, and you surely will not.

6. **Take a personal audit regularly, especially in the area of your thinking.** Go through the topics in this book on a regular basis like an MOT to see how you are doing. Find someone to give you a "check up" once a year to check for signs of early burnout.

7. **Have fun!** Think of the carefree life of a child (or at least how it should be). Stop trying to play God and being so serious about life. Learn to laugh. Be with energy-giving and fun-loving people on a regular basis. Do things that have nothing whatsoever to do with work or ministry. Develop a hobby. Life will go on while you take a break. Let God run the world and Jesus the church, and chill out. You will be a far greater blessing to other people if there is joy and laughter in your own soul.

You will not survive leadership if you allow yourself to get to the point of burnout.

Stop for a minute and consider:

1. **In the list above, how many suggestions are built into my life?**
2. **What danger signs of burnout have I experienced?**
3. **What do I need to do today to protect myself against burnout?**
4. **Am I living for the long haul or pacing myself?**

Notes

1. David Welch, Donald Medeiros & George Tate, *Beyond Burnout: How to Enjoy Your Job Again When You've Just About Had Enough,* Indiana, Prentice-Hall, 1982.
2. Beverley Potter, *Beating Job Burnout,* Oakland, Ronin Books, 1993.
3. M. Scott Peck, *The Road Less Travelled,* London, Arrow, 1990.

Conclusion

I met a young man recently who is the sales director in a large company. He told me that after a year of working for the company, he had an appraisal with the boss. The first question he was asked was, "Are you having fun?" The young man told me that it was then he realized why he wanted to go on working there. Of course it was important that he was doing a good job, but the boss's first concern was that he was enjoying it. He knew that a happy worker would probably be a good worker.

I know the ministry is hard and there are all sorts of things to discourage us, but at the end of the day we should love what we do. We are working for a good Boss! If the fun has gone we should reconsider how and what we are doing.

Here is the conclusion of Jerry Cook's poem (which we met in the introduction to this book):

Maybe if given a chance, and help
A person will emerge.
A day will come, I'm not sure just how,
When, without the corpse,
My love and I will laugh together again.
Laughter
Not strained or shallow.
"Being" laughter.
It just sort of bubbles out.
The kind of laughter people have
When they are... enjoying.

He found it again, and if you have lost it, you can as well.

I realize there will be things in this book that don't fit you, but in the main these issues affect most of us. We all need to be willing to make adjustments as we go along to ensure a good completion of the race.

I hope you will be full of vision and passion, and desire to see great things happening in the Kingdom of God in coming years, but I also hope you will be at peace, resting in the Lord and trusting him to do what he purposes to do. I trust you will get to the end of your ministry life free of regrets and with a great sense of joy in a race well run, knowing that to the best of your ability you did what you were asked and gifted to do.